Mel Bay's

ANTHOLOGY OF FINGERSTYLE GUITAR

by Tommy Flint

This text is a combination of years of study by Tommy Flint into various technics and styles used in contemporary and traditional fingerstyle guitar playing. We believe it to be the most thorough and complete guide to this popular and important style of guitar. This text contains carefully researched solo arrangements on music in styles ranging from blues to bluegrass, and from ragtime to country and gospel. It will be a definite addition to the library of any guitarist.

Visit us on the Web at www.melbay.com — E-mail us at email@melbay.com

Tommy Flint

To Fran, Travis, Kelly, and Patrick.

TYPES OF GUITARS
USED IN FINGER STYLE

FLAT TOP ACOUSTIC or FOLK   CLASSIC   HOLLOW BODY ELECTRIC   SOLID BODY ELECTRIC

GUITARS

FLAT TOP ACOUSTIC—This is a very versatile guitar and is widely used today. It can be adapted to almost any style of music from strumming folk songs to Travis picking, bluegrass, single string, and Chet Atkins style. It could possibly be considered the foundation of country music and the Nashville sound. It is possible to use almost any kind of strings on this type of guitar. Steel, bronze, silk, and steel or ball end nylon strings can be used. This guitar is characterized by the round sound hole and flat top.

CLASSIC GUITAR—The classic guitar is characterized by the round sound hole, wide neck and fingerboard, and nylon strings. The wood in a classic guitar is usually lighter than in other guitars in order to bring out the tone of the nylon strings. Never put steel strings on a classic guitar, because the wood will not be able to stand the stress or increased tension.

HOLLOW BODY ELECTRIC—This guitar is used in almost all styles of modern music from folk, rock, and jazz to country. The tone and quality is determined by the electrical pickup and amplifier control setting.

SOLID BODY ELECTRIC—This is the guitar found in most of today's rock music. The sound possibilities are unlimited depending on the pickup, amplifier and electronic devices used.

Both the acoustic and electric guitars are used by some of the greatest finger style guitarist. The type of guitar to use is strictly a matter of personal judgement as to which type would be best suited to the music being performed.

SEMI HOLLOW BODY ELECTRIC—This type of guitar is used a great deal in modern country music and rock. It has essentially the same possibilities as the solid body electric.

ARCH TOP ACOUSTIC—This type of guitar is not used a great deal in finger style playing, as the mellow wide tonal range of the round hole flat top is usually preferred. This instrument is used widely as a rhythm guitar in dance bands. The arch top and "F" holes produce a bright penetrating tone that "cuts" through the sound of the band.

SEMI HOLLOW BODY ELECTRIC   ARCH TOP ACCOUSTIC

STRINGS

NYLON STRINGS—Nylon strings are used on classic guitars. They have a soft mellow tone and are easy on the fingers. They stretch quite a bit and need to be tuned quite frequently. They will stay in tune much better after they have been on the guitar for a few days. Ball end nylon strings can also be used on flat top or folk guitars.

SILK AND STEEL—Silk and steel strings are excellent for finger style on the flat top folk guitar. They are usually easier on the fingers than the steel or bronze strings. They cannot be used on electric guitars as they will not pick up sufficiently.

STEEL STRINGS—Steel strings are used on the electric guitar. The wound strings are sometimes wound with nickel winding. We recommend fairly light gauge strings with a wound third for finger style on the electric guitar. Sometimes very light or slinky strings with a plain third are desirable for playing blues or rock on the solid body electric.

BRONZE—Bronze strings can be used on the flat top or folk guitar. They usually have greater volume and more brilliance then the silk and steel. The light gauge strings should be used for finger style unless you are using finger picks. Then it would be possible to use a heavier gauge. These strings should not be used on the electric guitar.

BRASS STRINGS—Brass strings are very similar to the bronze and are used for the same types of music. The tone is somewhat more sharp or bright. Brass strings are not to be used on the electric guitar.

FLAT WOUND—Flat wound strings are made for the electric guitar. They are wound with flat wire (no grooves or ridges) and are very smooth and soft to the touch. This also eliminates finger squeak (the finger sliding on the wound string). However, they do not have the brilliance of the round wound string.

FLAT POLISHED—Flat polished strings are standard wound strings which have been ground and polished until they are smooth. There are flat polished strings for both electric and acoustic guitars.

Again, the type of string for you is a matter of personal choice and depends of the tone desired for your preferred style and your requirements for ease of playing. The strings should be changed regularly in order to retain a good tone and accurate tuning. Old strings sound dead and will not tune true. The life of the string depends on how much you play and whether or not the strings are wiped clean after each playing session as well as the quality of the strings.

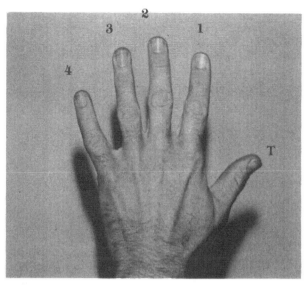

LEFT HAND

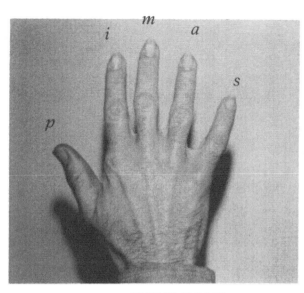

RIGHT HAND

Numbers for the left hand will appear in chord diagrams and above, below, or to the left of the notes in musical notation.

Fingers of the right hand will be indicated as follows:

> *p* — THUMB
> *i* — INDEX FINGER
> *m* — MIDDLE FINGER
> *a* — RING FINGER
> *s* — LITTLE FINGER

The letters to indicate the fingers will appear above, below, or to the right of the notes in musical notation and/or the numbers in tablature.

THE THUMB PICK

I would recommend using a thumb pick in order to get a clear ringing tone and also a good solid thump rhythm on the bass strings. This is especially important in the Atkins and Travis styles and also blues and ragtime. The thumb pick also is very useful in playing fast single string styles such as fiddle tunes and bluegrass. Down and up strokes.

Thumb picks come in many shapes and sizes. Most are plastic, however metal picks are available. Choosing the correct thumb pick is a matter of personal choice. I think most guitarists prefer the plastic pick. It is probably more adaptable to all styles of music.

Some people use no pick at all for playing accompaniment. Again, this is a matter of personal choice.

The thumb pick should fit on the thumb as shown in the photograph below. It should fit firm enough so as not to turn around on the thumb or slip off. However, it should not be tight enough to be uncomfortable.

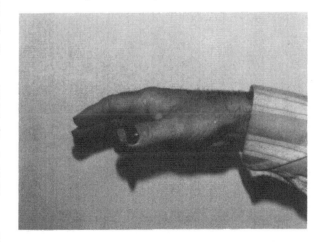

FINGER PICK

Finger Picks are *not* recommended. However they may be necessary on heavy gauge steel strings. For most people, finger picks seem to "get in the way" and limit the playing performance.

Although some very fine guitarists use finger picks, they have probably been playing for many years, or in some cases were banjo players before taking up the guitar. Again this is a matter of personal preference.

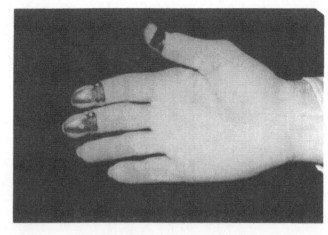

The finger picks go on the fingers as shown above. I have seen some guitarists use the picks on top of the fingers, over the nails and play down strokes. This seems to be very awkward and quite unnecessary.

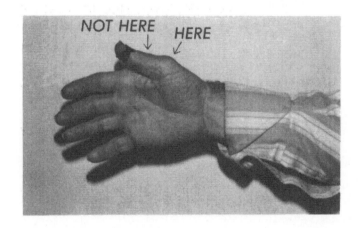

The thumb should *not* bend at the first joint. If you bend the thumb it will get in the way of your fingers and you will have very little control over it. The thumb should remain straight at all times.

RIGHT HAND POSITION

Let the hand "hang" in a relaxed position over the strings. Now place the thumb on either the fifth or sixth string, the index finger on the third string, middle finger on the second string, and the third finger on the first string. Now your hand is in the proper playing position. This may vary with different styles, but basically this is the correct position. Remember to relax.

The wrist should remain stationary at all times when playing finger style. Use the fingers only. Just curl them in toward the palm of the hand as if making a loose fist.

REMEMBER — DO NOT USE THE WRIST

6

THE RIGHT HAND

The right hand before picking the string.

The right hand in the closed fist position after plucking the strings.

FINGERNAILS

LEFT HAND

The fingernails of the left hand should be filed very short so as not to interfere with holding down the strings and making chords. They should also be very smooth so they won't hang up on the string and cause sloppy technique.

RIGHT HAND

The nails on the right hand should be filed to the approximate shape or contour of the finger tips. They should extend slightly past the finger tips. (approx. 1/16) It is advisable to carry an emoryboard to keep the nails smooth and in playing condition.

Generally speaking, it is not wise to play heavy steel or bronze strings with the bare fingers. You may wear the nail down, and cause gaps and notches to appear in them.

THE LEFT HAND POSITION

Place the fingers firmly on the strings very close to the frets. Bend the fingers and use the finger tips unless you are holding down more than one string with the same finger. Then the finger should lay flat on the fingerboard. Generally, the ball or pad (never the tip) of the thumb should remain on the back of the guitar neck. Do not bend the thumb. Occasionally it may be necessary to use the thumb on the bass string on some chords. In this case it will obviously be essential that you bend the thumb.

If the strings buzz or rattle, slide the fingers up closer to the frets. Remember to keep the fingers arched so they will not touch other strings and deaden them.

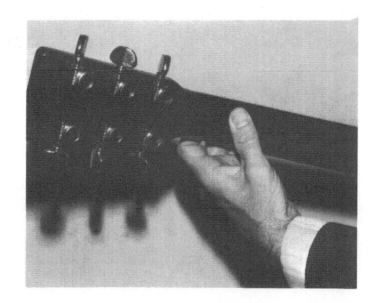

The correct position of the thumb.

Remember to keep the fingers arched.

Position of the left hand when using the thumb on the bass.

CHORD DIAGRAMS

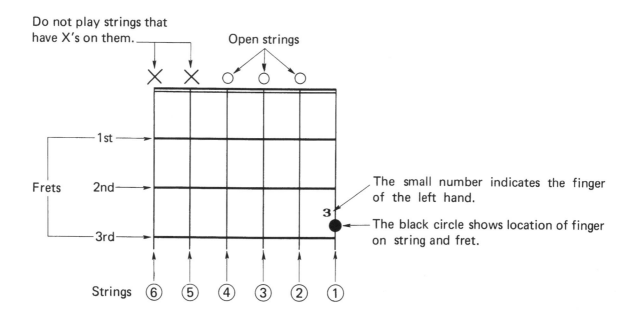

Do not play strings that have X's on them.

Open strings

1st

Frets

2nd

3rd

The small number indicates the finger of the left hand.

The black circle shows location of finger on string and fret.

Strings ⑥ ⑤ ④ ③ ② ①

The vertical lines are the strings. The horizontal lines are the frets. The encircled numerals are the string numbers.

Open string = Do not touch string with the left hand.
Do pick string with the right hand.

HOW TO FINGER CHORDS

When making a chord, the fingers should be arched so the finger tips are pressing the strings straight in toward the finger board. Care should be taken that a finger does not touch any string other than the one it is depressing. The fingers should be placed firmly on the strings (as close to the frets as possible without getting directly on them.)

9

TUNING THE GUITAR

If you are a beginner, it would be logical to have someone — your instructor or a friend who plays, tune the instrument for you. The knack of tuning the guitar accurately is in most cases acquired after the student has been playing for a period of time. A great deal of experimentation, practice and patience will be required until the ear has developed to a point where it is capable of determining the exact pitch of the strings.

There are various methods of tuning such as: by octaves, harmonics, chord inversions etc. The three most common methods are shown below.

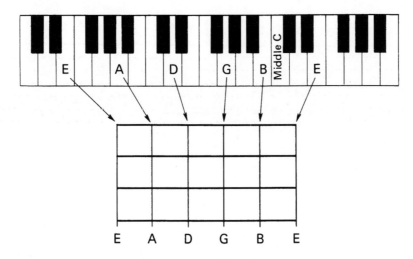

The six open strings of the guitar are the same pitch as the six notes shown on the piano keyboard. The first string is above middle C. The other five strings are below middle C.

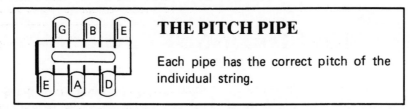

THE PITCH PIPE

Each pipe has the correct pitch of the individual string.

If both piano and pitch pipe are unavailable:

1. Tighten the 6th string until you get a good clear tone.
2. Place the finger on the 6th string behind the 5th fret. This will give you the pitch of the open 5th string.
3. Place the finger on the 5th string behind the 5th fret to get the pitch of the open 4th string.
4. Place the finger on the 4th string 5th fret to get the pitch of the open 3rd string.
5. Place the finger on the 3rd string behind the 4th fret to obtain the pitch of the open 2nd string.
6. Place the finger on the 2nd string behind the 5th fret to obtain the tone of the open 1st string.

Now the guitar should be in fairly good tune and the chords will sound pleasing to the ear.

10

YOU DO NOT HAVE TO BE ABLE TO READ MUSIC
To Use This Book

You do not have to be able to read music to use this book, as all examples, exercises and solos are written in the easy and convenient tablature or diagram form. If you do read music, it is still recommended that you learn this handy system.

How to Read Tablature
The Fingerboard

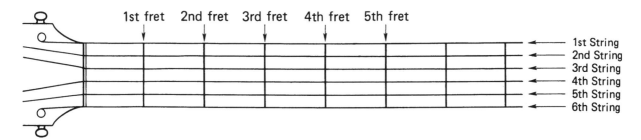

Tablature

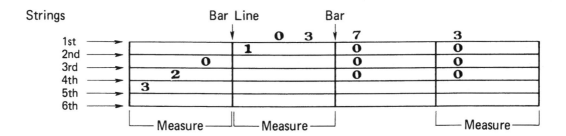

The lines represent the strings of the guitar. The numbers represent the frets. O indicates open string. When a number is above the top line, it will be played on the first string. When a number is above the second line from the top, it will be played on the second string, etc.

In the example above, the number three in the first measure indicates the third fret on the fifth string. The number two indicates the second fret on the fourth string. The O indicates the third string open.

In the third measure, the number seven indicates the seventh fret on the first string. The second, third, and fourth strings are open. The four strings will be struck simultaneously as a chord. When the numbers are arranged vertically they are always played simultaneously.

A small curved line between the numbers indicates they are to be counted as eighth notes. In other words, the first number is on the count and the latter number is on the "AND" or half way between the counts.

EIGHTH NOTES

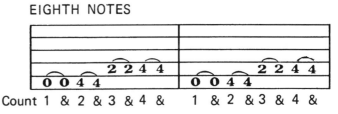

For sixteenth note rhythm the curved line will arch over four numbers.

YOU DO NOT HAVE TO READ MUSIC TO USE THIS BOOK

However it would be wise to learn the meaning of some of the symbols that are used in tablature as well as musicial notation some of these symbols are time signatures (how to keep time), tempo (rate of speed), repeat signs, endings, etc. Some of the most commonly used signs are shown on this page.

TIME SIGNATURES

The $\frac{2}{4}$, $\frac{4}{4}$, $\frac{3}{4}$ or $\frac{6}{8}$ at the beginning of a piece of music are called the time signatures. The upper numeral tells you how many beats or counts are in each measure. 𝄴 means common time or the same as $\frac{4}{4}$.

𝄵 is Alla Breve or cut time which in this book is the same as $\frac{2}{4}$

Repeat Signs

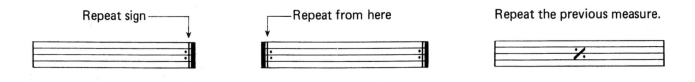

Repeat sign ———   Repeat from here   Repeat the previous measure.

D.C. repeat from the beginning.   D.S. repeat from the 𝄋 sign.
D.C. al Fine. repeat from the beginning and end at Fine.
D.S. al Coda. repeat from 𝄋   Play to the sign 𝄌   Then go to the Coda.

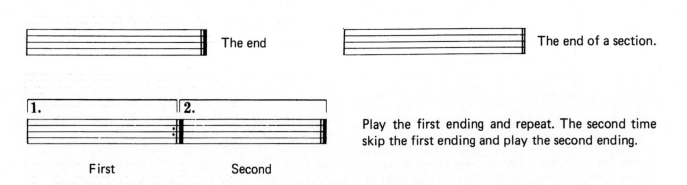

The end   The end of a section.

1.   **2.**   Play the first ending and repeat. The second time skip the first ending and play the second ending.

First   Second

The Arpeggio Sign

The wavy line placed before a chord means to strum slowly over the chord from the lowest note to the highest, producing a harplike effect.

HOW TO KEEP TIME

The $\frac{2}{4}$, $\frac{3}{4}$ or $\frac{4}{4}$ at the beginning of an exercise or solo is called the time signature. The top number tells you how many counts are in each measure. $\mathbf{C}$ means common time or the same as $\frac{4}{4}$. $\mathbf{\phi}$ is cut time. In this book it will mean the same as $\frac{2}{4}$.

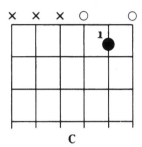

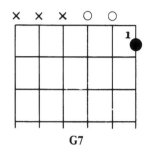

Make the little "one" finger C chord. Place the thumb of the right hand on the third string and in one quick movement bring the thumb down, striking the third, second, and first strings in one stroke. Use this method to play the following exercises.

Use the thumb only. Strum four beats in every measure. Space the notes very evenly. Count aloud.

Practice until mastered

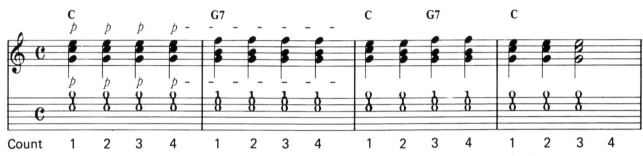

Strum three beats per measure

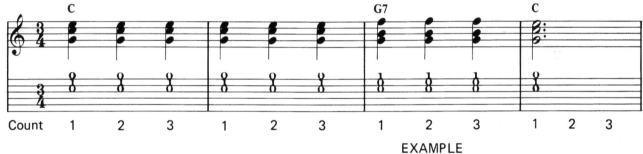

In the Tabulature, a curved line between two chords or notes indicates that there is an "and" after the count. The "and" should be played exactly half way between the counts.

EXAMPLE

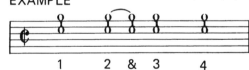

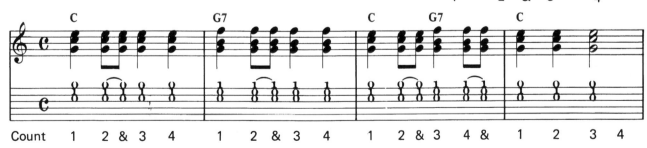

13

THE CHORDS USED IN THIS SECTION
Major Chords

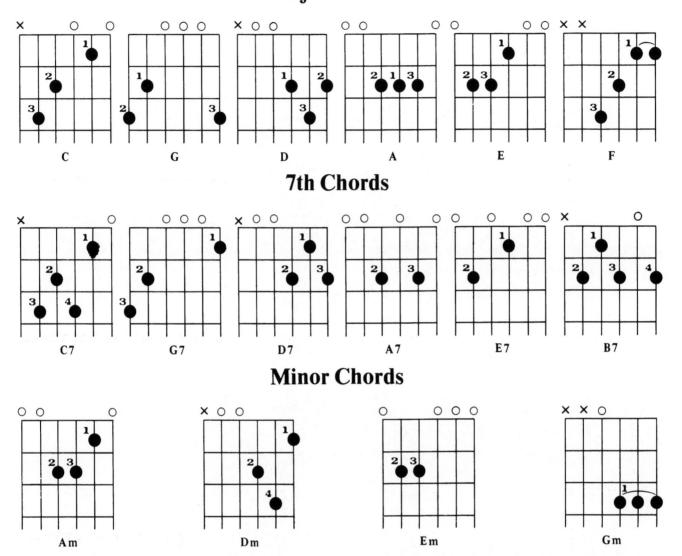

7th Chords

Minor Chords

If you are unfamiliar with any of the chords on this page, I would suggest that you practice playing the three principal chords in the basic "Open String" keys. The principal chords are simply the three most commonly used chords in a given key. They just seem to fit together and sound very plesant to the ear. Knowing how the chords fit together is an invaluable asset when playing by ear. It eliminates much of the guesswork and saves a great deal of time.

The three principal chords are called:

the TONIC   SUB. DOMINANT and DOMINANT 7th

or the 1   4   and   5 Chords

It is very easy to find the three principal chords on the chord circle on the following page.

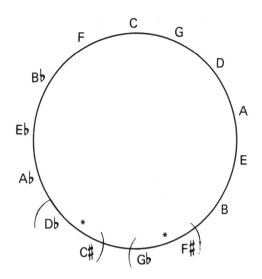

HOW TO FIND THE CHORDS

The three principal chords are:

           TONIC   SUB DOMINANT and DOMINANT 7TH
    or   1   4   and   5

Pick out any chord on the circle. This is the tonic chord. Now move counterclockwise to the next chord. This is the sub dominant chord.

The first chord clockwise to the tonic is the dominant 7th chord.

The dominant 7th naturally is a seventh chord.

As an example the chords in the key of C are C, F and G7.

In the key of G: G, C and D7 or the key of E: E, A and B7.

You now know enough chords to play in the keys of C, G, D, A and E.

How To Practice

Play the tonic, sub dom. dom. 7th and tonic. Use the thumb and strum each chord four beats spacing the counts as evenly as a clock.

Example

Each diagonal line represents a strum with the thumb.

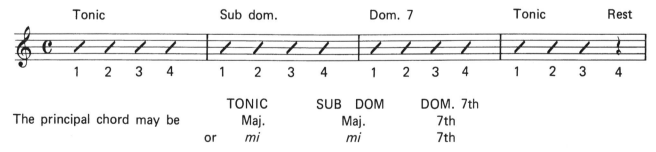

The principal chord may be

	TONIC	SUB DOM	DOM. 7th
	Maj.	Maj.	7th
or	mi	mi	7th

* The fingering for D♭ and C♯ is identical. Also G♭ and F♯ are identical.

15

THE BASIC THUMB AND FINGER STYLE

Sometimes called the **Drop Thumb** or **Country Lick.**

This basic rhythm can provide a beautiful background for many country and folk songs.

At this point it is assumed that you know the basic chords and have acquired the facility for changing them in an easy flowing manner.

1. Hold C chord with the left hand
2. Place the thumb of the right hand on the ⑤ string. (figure 1)
3. The fingers should be curled in toward the palm, as if making a loose fist. (figure 2)
4. Now, move the thumb in a downward motion picking the ⑤ string
5. Next, rapidly straighten the *index* finger, striking three or four strings (preferably the first three) with the back of the nail. (figure 3)

6. Slowly and evenly say Oom Pah Oom Pah. When you say **Oom** pluck the bass string with the thumb. When you say **Pah** strike the chord (first three strings) with the back of the *index* fingernail.
7. Now make G7 chord and repeat this pattern, except, pick the ⑥ string with the thumb. (bass note)
8. Practice changing C and G7 chords while playing this pattern. Keep a steady even rhythm.

The Country Lick Example

Say Oom Pah Oom Pah Oom Pah Oom Pah
or Count 1 2 3 4   1 2   3 4

Now shall we apply the basic lick to a song?

The melody line will be written in its entirety in both musicial notation and tablature so the guitarist who is unfamiliar with the song will be able to learn the tune. The accompaniment or rhythm pattern will be used throughout the entire song. Chord symbols will be written above the melody line to show you where to change chords. Play a steady Oom Pah Oom Pah rhythm and sing the words in a flowing relaxed manner.

The accompaniment pattern

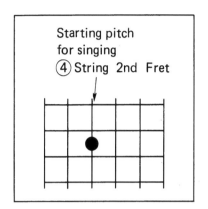

Starting pitch for singing
④ String 2nd Fret

Oom Pah Oom Pah
or 1   2   3   4

GO TELL AUNT RHODY
(The Old Grey Goose Is Dead)

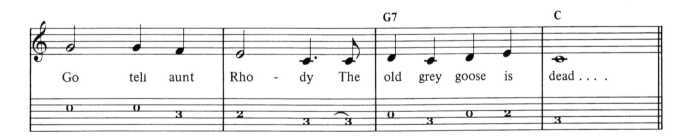

C / / / ////
2. The one that she's been saving
G7 / / / C///
The one that she's been saving
C / / / ////
The one that she's been saving
G7 / / / C ///
To make a feather bed

3. She died in the mill pond
   She died in the mill pond
   She died in the mill pond
   With a stone upon her head.

Now let's play the basic drop thumb style in a different key.

The rhythm is exactly the same: Oom Pah Oom Pah

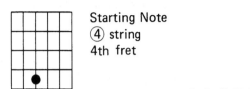

Starting Note
④ string
4th fret

The thumb will play:
The ④ string in D chord.
The ⑥ string in G chord.
The ⑤ string A7

GOODNIGHT LADIES

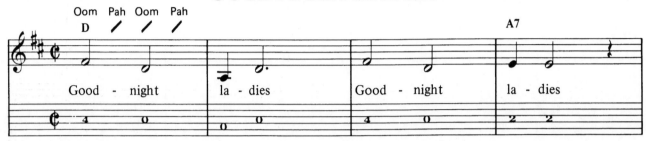

MERRILY WE ROLL ALONG

Starting Pitch
④ String
4 Fret

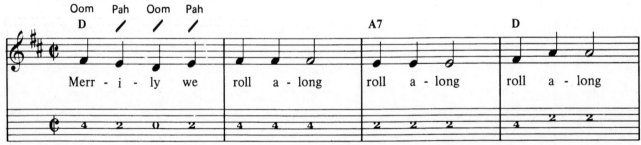

18

ALTERNATE BASS NOTES

The use of alternate bass notes will spice up the rhythm pattern and add a bit of color to the background.

How to play alternate basses on the drop thumb style.

The pattern is the same except when you are in C chord Move the third finger to the ⑥ string, third fret on the second Oom or the count of three and pick this note with the thumb. Do not move the other fingers.

When you are in G7 chord the alternate bass note is the ④ string open.

Example

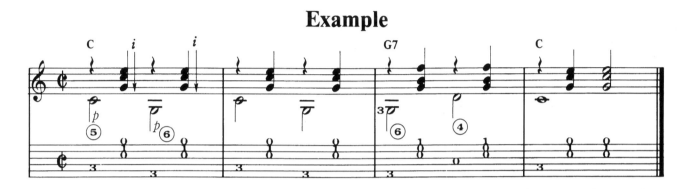

SKIP TO MY LOU

With Alternate Bass Notes

Starting Note

④ string
2nd fret

2. Flies in the butter milk, shoo fly shoo
   Flies in the butter milk, shoo fly shoo
   Flies in the butter milk, shoo fly shoo
   Skip to my Lou my darling

3. Lost my partner what'll I do?
   Lost my partner what'll I do?
   Lost my partner what'll I do?
   Skip to my Lou my darling.

ALTERNATE BASS NOTE CHART

■ = Root   ▲ = Alternate Bass   □ = Root on open string   △ = Open alternate

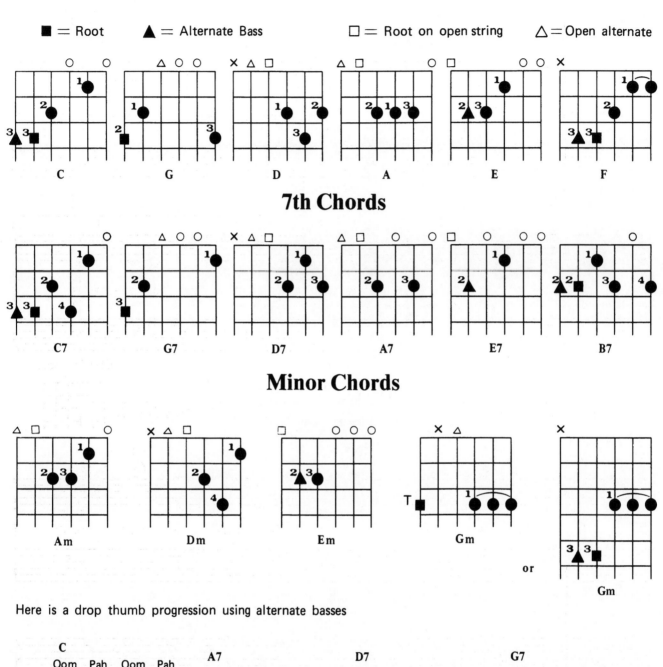

7th Chords

Minor Chords

Here is a drop thumb progression using alternate basses

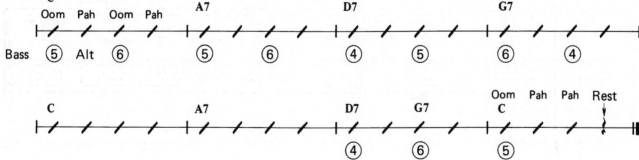

BURY ME NOT ON THE LONE PRAIRIE

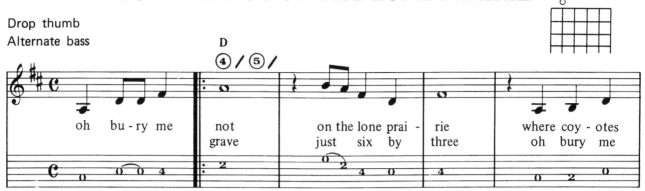

HE'S GOT THE WHOLE WORLD IN HIS HANDS

Repeat each first line two times.

2. He's got the little bitty baby
   in His hands.
   He's got the whole world
   in His hands.

3. He got you and me brother,
   in His hands
   He got the whole world in
   His hands.

4. He's got the wind and the rain
   in his hands
   He's got the whole world
   in his hands.

THE DROP THUMB DOUBLE STRUM

This is very similar to the basic thumb and finger style. In fact, it is the same except the thumb plays once and the finger plays twice. (down and up.) This style provides a more full background.

An easy way to keep time is to simply say "Boom Chick A" "Boom Chick A". Pick the bass string with the thumb on **"Boom."** On **"Chick"** strike the first three strings (a down stroke with the back of the index finger nail.) On **"A"** curl the index finger in and play an up stroke on the first three strings.

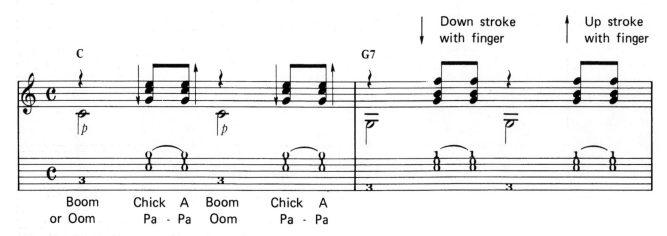

Remember the **"A"** is half way between **"Chick"** and **"Boom"** or **"Pah"** and **"Oom"**.

The drop thumb double strum with alternate basses.

Example

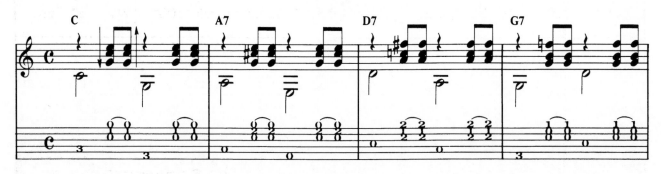

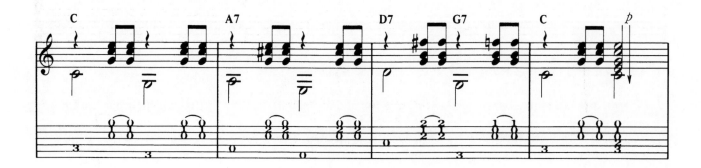

22

HAND ME DOWN MY WALKING CANE

Starting tone

Drop thumb double strum
Alternate bass

Hand me down ... my walk - ing cane _____ Hand me

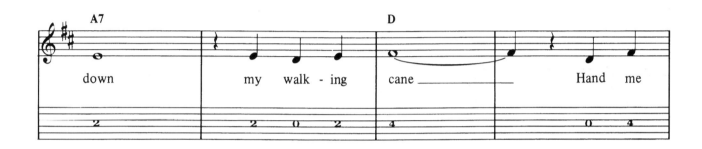

down ... my walk - ing cane _____ Hand me

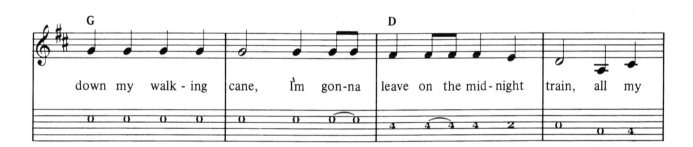

down my walk - ing cane, I'm gon-na leave on the mid-night train, all my

sins been tak-en a - way tak-en a - way _____

Verse   I got drunk, and I got in jail
I got drunk, and I got in jail
I got drunk, and I got in jail
Had no one to go my bail

All my sins been taken away, taken away
Chorus

THE BASIC FOLK STYLE

Now, instead of simply striking the strings with the nail, we will begin picking or plucking the strings with the fingers.

Place the right hand in the following position.

1. Thumb on the ④ string
2. Index finger on the ③ string.
3. Middle finger on the ② string.
4. Third finger on the ① string.

The hand should hang in a relaxed manner. Do not move the wrist. Use the thumb and fingers only.

Now form a D chord with the left hand.

HOW TO PLAY

Pick the fourth string with the thumb. Next curl the fingers in toward the palm as if making a loose fist and pick the third, second, and first strings simultaneously.

Now repeat this exercise until a steady Oom pah Oom pah rhythm has been obtained.

Remember to use the fingers only and don't tense up.

RELAX!

It would be a good idea to play the three principal chords in all keys using alternate bass notes on the basic folk style.

Ready to play

Fingers in closed position after playing

Example

SOURWOOD MOUNTAIN

Starting Note

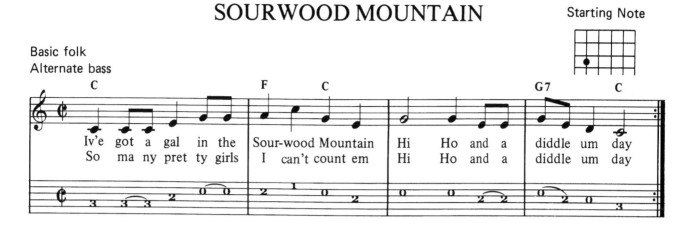

Basic folk
Alternate bass

Iv'e got a gal in the | Sour-wood Mountain | Hi Ho and a | diddle um day
So ma ny pret ty girls | I can't count em | Hi Ho and a | diddle um day

Starting note

THIS TRAIN

Basic folk
Alternate bass

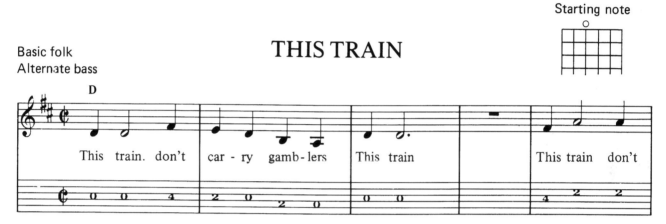

This train. don't | car - ry gamb-lers | This train | | This train don't

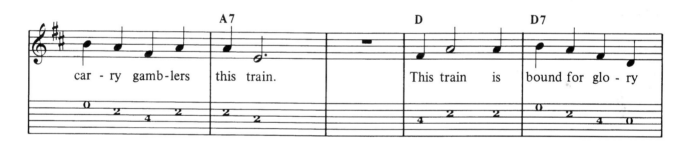

car - ry gamb-lers | this train. | | This train is | bound for glo - ry

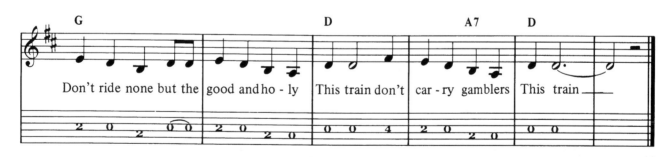

Don't ride none but the | good and ho - ly | This train don't | car - ry gamblers | This train___

2. This train don't carry liars, this train
   This train don't carry liars, this train
   This train is bound for glory
   Dont carry none but the good and holy
   This train don't carry liars, this train.

3. This train is bound for glory, this train
   This train is bound for glory, this train
   This train is bound for glory
   Don't carry none but the good and holy
   This train is bound for glory, this train.

LITTLE BROWN JUG

Basic folk
Alternate bass

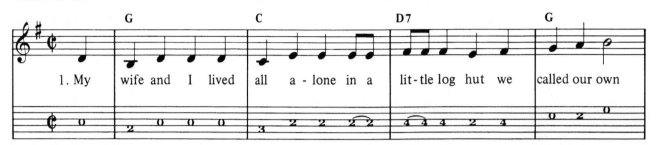

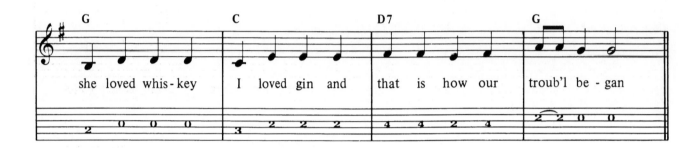

Chorus

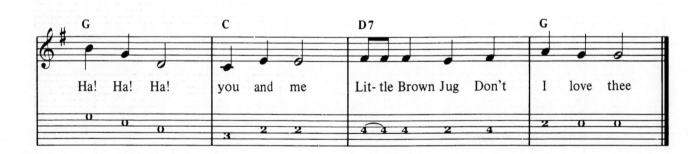

2. When I go toiling on my farm
   I tote my brown jug under my arm
   I put it under a shady tree
   Oh little brown, you and me

   Chorus

3. My wife and I and a little Brown dog,
   Crossed the river on a hollow log
   The log did break, the dog fell in,
   I got in the water clear up to my chin.

   Chorus

THE BASIC FOLK STYLE IN $\frac{3}{4}$ TIME

In $\frac{3}{4}$ time (sometimes called waltz time) there are three beats to the measure. The count would be one, two, three, or you can say Boom, Chick, Chick. The thumb will play the bass string on Boom and the fingers will pluck the third, second and first strings on Chick, Chick. Space the beats evenly.

Example

BASIC $\frac{3}{4}$ WITH A MOVING BASS LINE

The moving bass line can enhance the beauty of some songs. In the following song the encircled numeral indicates the bass string to be plucked with the thumb. The rhythm is Boom Chick chick.

THE STREETS OF LAREDO

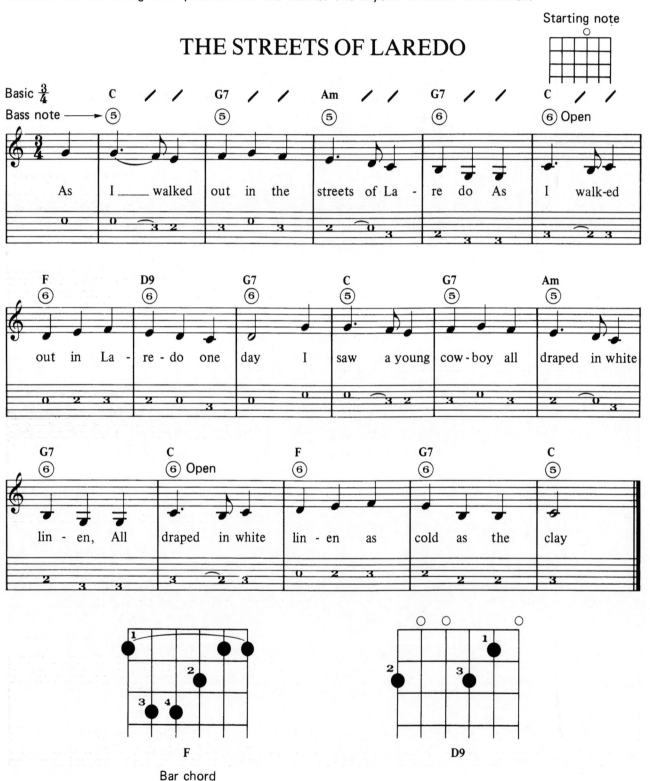

Bar chord

THREE FINGER ROLLS

The three finger rolls are in eighth note rhythm, or in other words the picking is doubled or twice as fast as the Boom-Chick quarter note rhythm. The count is Boom-a-Chick-a-Boom-a-Chick-a.

Make C chord and play this pattern.	Picking	p	i	a m 1 2	i	p	i	a m 1 2	i
	String	⑤	③	①②	③	④	③	①②	③
	Count	Boom-A-Chick-A				Boom-A-Chick-A			
	or	1	&	2	&	3	&	4	&

Space the notes evenly. The A is half way between boom and chick. The first and second string are picked simultaneously on the chicks or the counts of two and four.

No. 1

or 1 & 2 & 3 & 4 &
The count is Boom-a-Chick-a-Chick-a-

No. 2

No. 3

The count is the same as the previous pattern. However the picking is different. This pattern moves from the p to i and $\frac{a}{m}$ and does not come back to the i as the above patterns. It has a syncopated feel.

29

GREEN GROW THE LILACS

Starting note

Three finger roll no. 2
Alternate basses

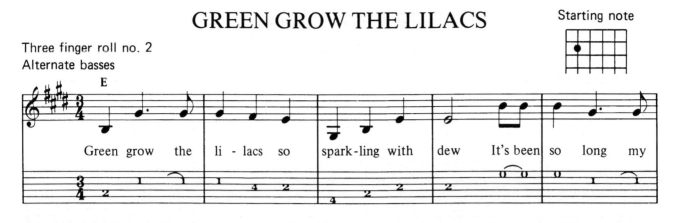

Green grow the li - lacs so spark-ling with dew It's been so long my

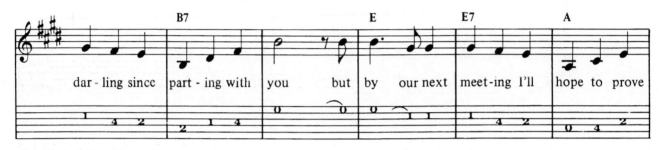

dar - ling since part - ing with you but by our next meet-ing I'll hope to prove

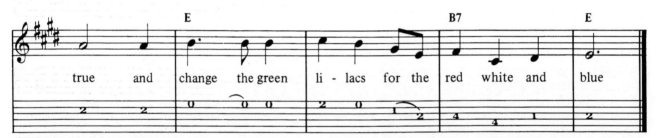

true and change the green li - lacs for the red white and blue

2. I used to have a sweetheart
   But now I have none,
   Since she's gone and left me I care not for one.
   Since she's gone and left me contented I'll be
   For she loves another one better than me.

3. I passed my love's window both early and late
   The look that she gave me it made my heart ache
   On the look that she gave me was painful to see
   For she loves another one better than me.

The Combination

This pattern is a combination of the basic folk style and the three finger roll No 1. The first half of the measure is the basic folk. The last half is the roll The count is Boom-Chick-Boom-a-Chick-a or Oom-Pah-Oom-Pa-Pa-Pa. Alternate basses.

THE ERIE CANAL

The encircled numerals indicate bass strings in chorus

Starting note

Moderate combination
Alternate bases on verse

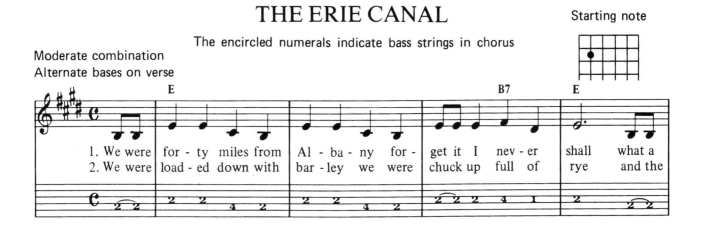

1. We were for-ty miles from Al-ba-ny for-get it I nev-er shall what a
2. We were load-ed down with bar-ley we were chuck up full of rye and the

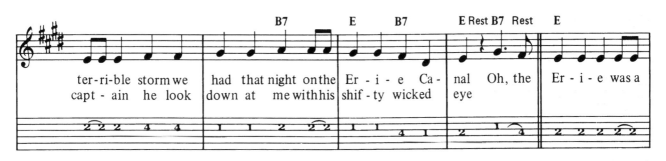

ter-ri-ble storm we had that night on the Er-i-e Ca-nal Oh, the Er-i-e was a
capt-ain he look down at me with his shif-ty wicked eye

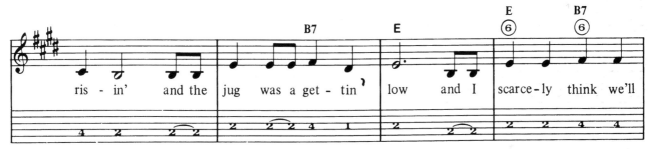

ris-in' and the jug was a get-tin' low and I scarce-ly think we'll

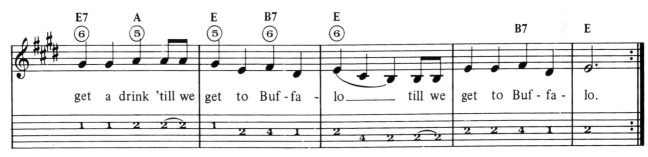

get a drink 'till we get to Buf-fa-lo till we get to Buf-fa-lo.

Used in measure no. 14

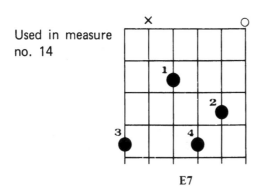

E7

31

THE LATIN ROLL

This pattern is the same at the three finger roll No. 3, except there are two additional strokes at the end of every measure (on the count of four.) The easiest way to count the time is "Boom-a-Chick-a-Boom-a-Chick-a" or "Oom-Pa-Pa-Pa-Oom-Pa-Pa-Pa." Space the beats very evenly. This rhythm can be played at any tempo. Fast or slow.

Example

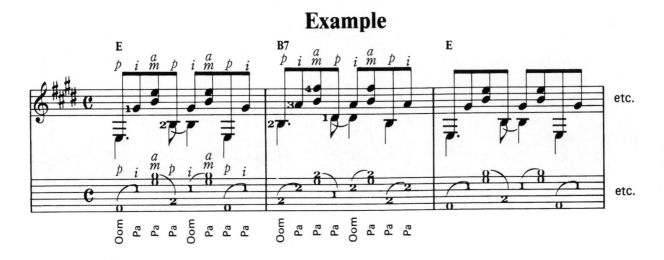

In The Key of D

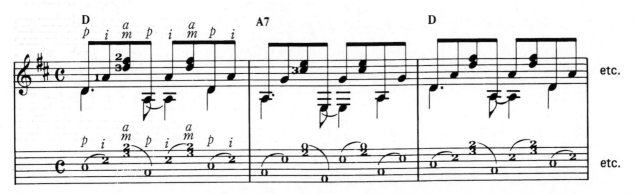

A Chord Progression

32

THE LATIN ROLL VARIATIONS

The sequence of notes in this roll can be played in any order forward or backward, beginning with the thumb (*p*) index (*i*) or middle and third (*m a*) fingers. The acent is felt when the thumb plays the bass string. Each time the picking pattern is changed, the accents are shifted to new or different positions in the measure. Therefore, each pattern has a different feel. Practice each pattern eight or ten times in succession.

Forward Rolls

Basic

Var. I

Var. II

Backward Rolls

Backward

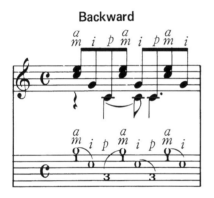

Var. I

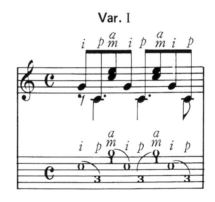

Var. II

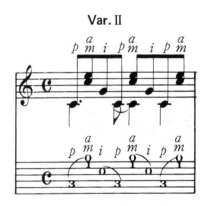

The Continuous Roll

This is actually an uninterrupted flow of the *p, i, $\frac{a}{m}$* roll. The pattern repeats itself every fourth measure. The continuous backward roll is an unbroken flow of the $\frac{a}{m}$, *i, p* roll.

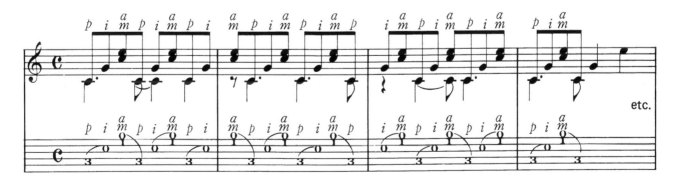

LA CUCARACHA

Starting tone

Play a couple of measures of rhythm to set the tempo before beginning the song.

Moderately bright
Latin Roll

Now my girl here in the coun - try__ she's a ver - y love-ly miss__

and the girls out in Del- rio __ they al - ways give me kiss.__ La - cu.-ca

Chours

rach - a,__ la cu - ca - rach - a __ now we have to tra-vel on __ la cu - ca

rach - a __ la cu - ca - rach - a __ Pan-choVil - las men are coming.

ARPEGGIO STYLE

The term "Arpeggio" means to play the notes of a chord consecutively. To play arpeggio accompaniment, make C chord and place the right hand on the strings as shown in the photograph. Beginning with the bass or lowest tone, play the notes of the chord *(p, i, m, a,)* in a steady even eighth note rhythm. Play slowly and evenly. Count 1 and 2 and 3 and 4 and or say Oom-Pa-Pa-Pa-Oom-Pa-Pa-Pa.

Arpeggio style accompaniment can provide a beautiful background for ballads, hymns, or songs with a great deal of expression.

p on the ⑤ string
i on the ③ string
m on the ② string
a on the ① string

Arpeggio Style

The Broken Arpeggio

AURA LEE

With expression
Broken arpeggio
Slowly

Starting note

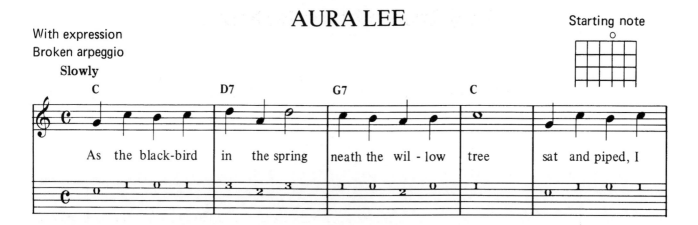

As the black-bird in the spring neath the wil - low tree sat and piped, I

Begin 3 finger roll No. 1

heard him sing praise of Au - ra Lee Au - ra Lee Au - Ra Lee maid of gold - en

Roll No 1

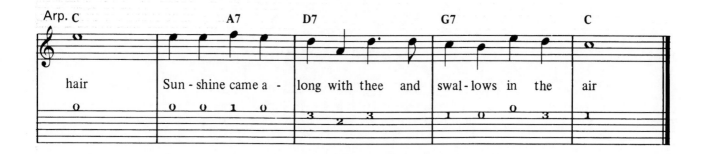

hair Sun - shine came a - long with thee and swal - lows in the air

The 3/4 Arpegio Style
Example

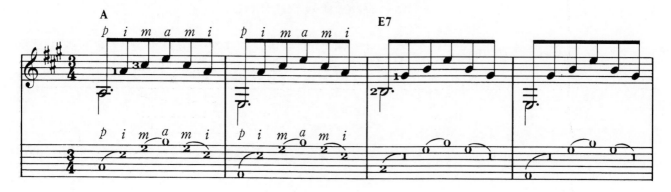

36

The $\frac{3}{4}$ Broken Arpeggio Example

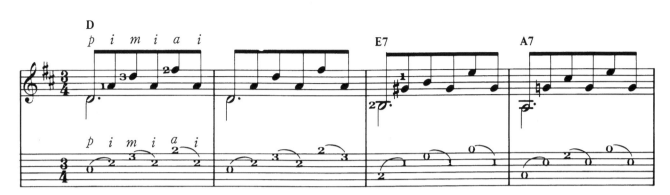

DOWN IN THE VALLEY

Starting note

$\frac{3}{4}$ Broken arpeggio
Alternate basses

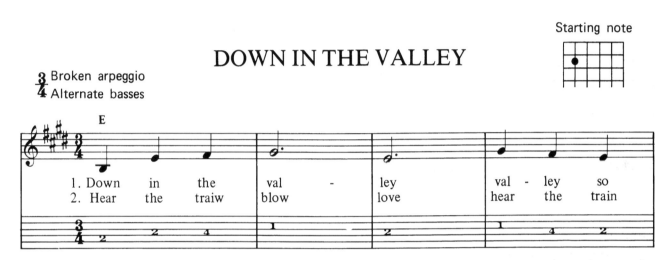

1. Down in the val - ley val - ley so
2. Hear the traiw blow love hear the train

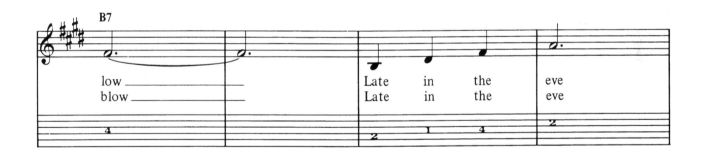

low ___ Late in the eve
blow ___ Late in the eve

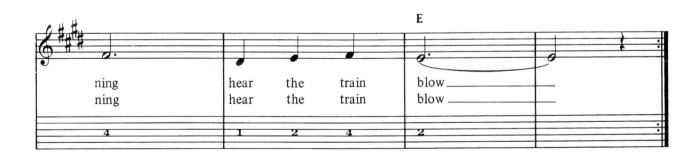

ning hear the train blow ___
ning hear the train blow ___

HOW TO PLAY IN $\frac{6}{8}$ TIME

Six eight time means there are six beats,to the measure. The accents are on the first and fourth beats. Slow six eight accompaniment can be played by using a three four pattern and doubling each measure.

Basic $\frac{6}{8}$ Accompaniment

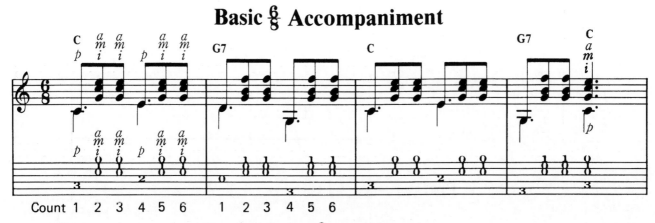

Count 1 2 3 4 5 6   1 2 3 4 5 6

Silent Night is a very good example of a song using $\frac{6}{8}$ accompaniment.

SILENT NIGHT

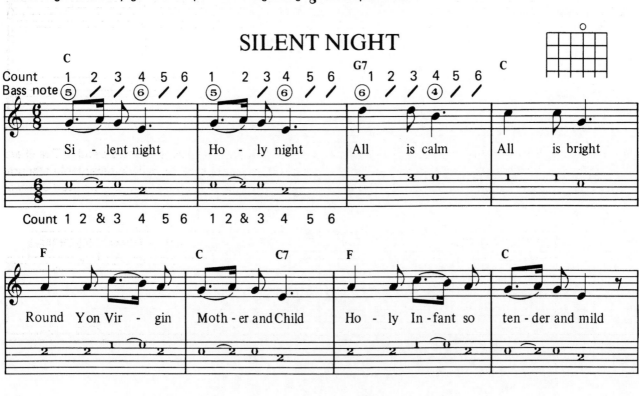

38

THE SLOW $\frac{6}{8}$ ARPEGGIO

The slow $\frac{6}{8}$ arpeggio is played the same as the $\frac{3}{4}$ arpeggio, with the exception of the measures being doubled. (Twice as many notes in each measure.)

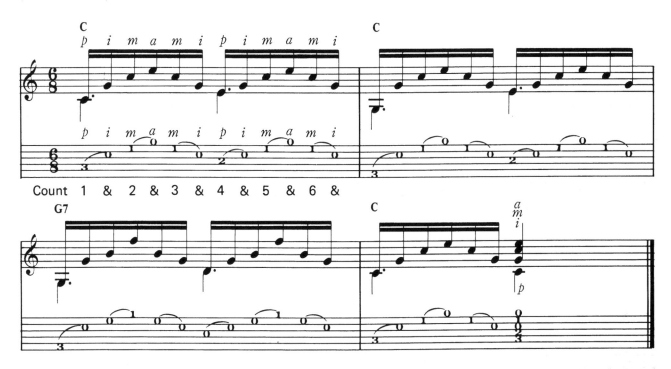

Count 1 & 2 & 3 & 4 & 5 & 6 &

Now let us sing Silent Night with the arpeggio accompaniment. Be sure to space the notes evenly. The chart below shows where the syllables or words fall into place in the arpeggio pattern. With a reasonable amount of practice I believe that you will be able to feel the natural flow of the rhythm within a short period of time.

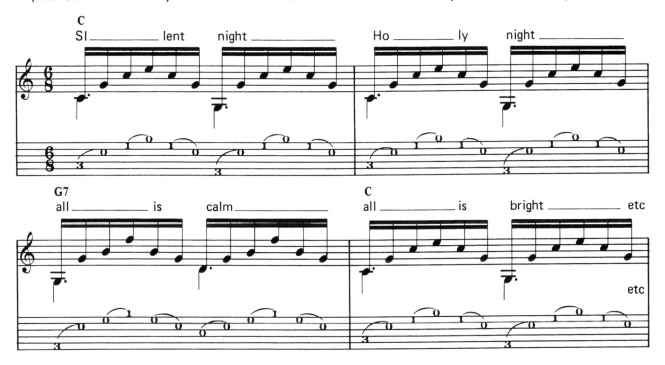

MODERATE AND FAST $\frac{6}{8}$ ACCOMPANIMENT

In fast $\frac{6}{8}$ rhythm the accents are still on the counts of one and four. However, we do not play on every count. Perhaps the easiest accompaniment is the basic $\frac{6}{8}$ strum. The thumb picks the bass string on the counts of one and four. The fingers pluck the chord on the counts of three and six. This style seems easier played if counted in a "two beat" rhythm. The count would be 1-and-a-2-and-a. The fast $\frac{6}{8}$ would be counted 1-ah-2-ah-1-ah-2-ah. I have heard it counted Humpt-ty-Dump-ty-Hump-ty-Dump-ty.

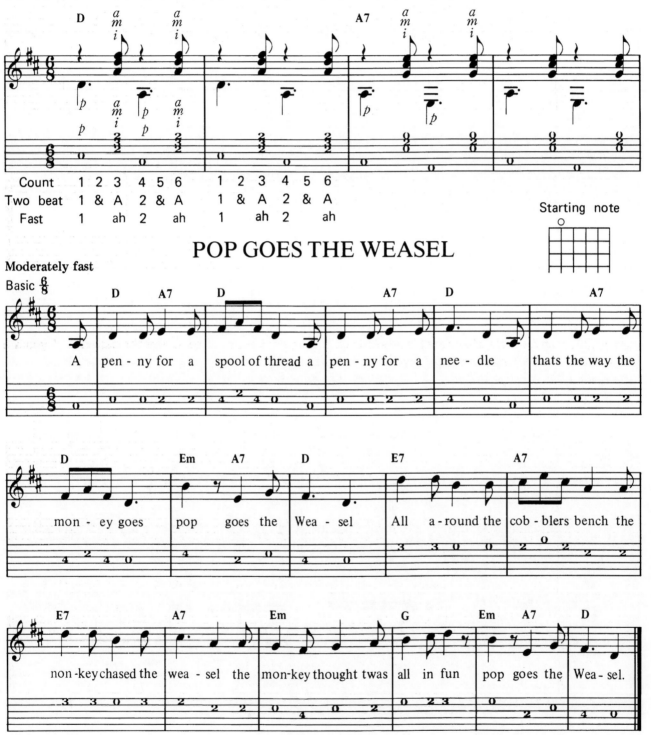

Count	1	2	3		4	5	6		1	2	3		4	5	6
Two beat	1	&	A		2	&	A		1	&	A		2	&	A
Fast	1		ah		2		ah		1		ah		2		ah

Starting note

POP GOES THE WEASEL

Moderately fast
Basic $\frac{6}{8}$

A pen - ny for a spool of thread a pen - ny for a nee - dle thats the way the

mon - ey goes pop goes the Wea - sel All a - round the cob - blers bench the

non - key chased the wea - sel the mon - key thought twas all in fun pop goes the Wea - sel.

40

BASS RUNS

Bass runs are usually made up of passing tones between the chords. They can be used to lead into new phrases, or different sections as verse to chorus.

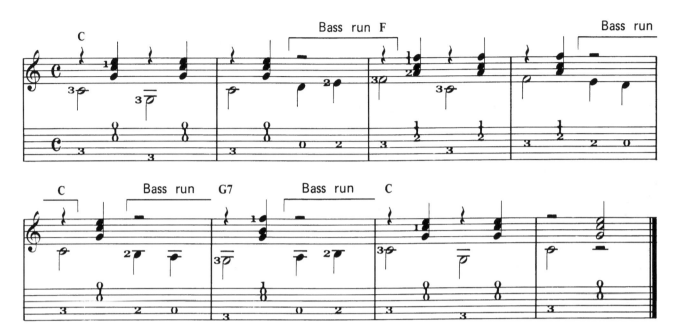

LITTLE BROWN JUG

In the following example, the accompaniment is written to demonstrate the use of the bass run. If you are unfamiliar with the melody, refer to page 26.

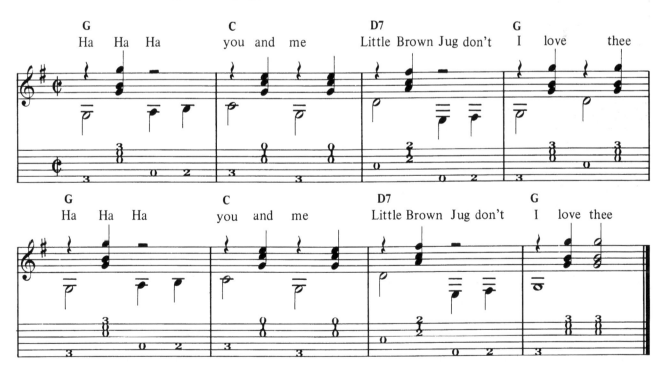

The first five examples show how the bass run can be used in changing from to **Tonic** to the **Sub. Dominant,** or from the Dominant to the Tonic. In the second case, the first chord in the example would be a seventh chord and would resolve to the tonic. (Major). The last five examples show the bass run changing from Tonic to Dom. 7. or Sub. Dom to Tonic.

* In the last case the second chord in the example would be a major chord. (Tonic)

SOME ACCOMPANIMENT PATTERNS

The following patterns are divided into four sections "Picks and Strums," "Arpeggios' and Rolls," "Combinations" and "Latin Rhythms." This is not a complete index as no book will be totally complete as long as there are creative guitarist around. However, it is hoped that you will gain some knowledge of the types of rhythms and acquire good taste for selecting the "Right" accompaniment. The pattern to use with a particular song is a matter of personal preference and taste. With a bit of experimentation you will find the right one.

For the sake of convenience only C chord is used in the following examples. Any pattern can be applied to any chord or chord progression.

Picks And Strums

1. Boom Chick Boom Chick
2. Boom Chick Boom Chick-a
3. Boom Chick-A Boom Chick
4. Boom Chick-a Boom Chick-a
5. Boom-a Chick-a Boom-a Chick-a
6. Boom-a Chick-a Boom-a Chick-a
7. Boom Chick Chick Chick-a
8. Boom-a Chick-a Boom-a Chick-a
9. Boom Chick Boom Chick
10. Boom Chick Chick
11. Boom Chick-a Chick-a
12. Boom Chick Chick-a

ARPEGGIOS AND ROLLS

Common time

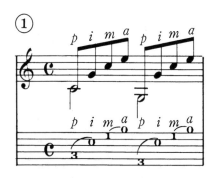
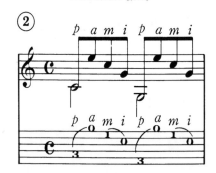
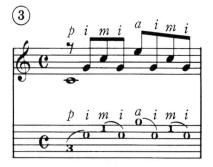

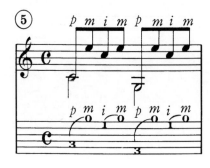
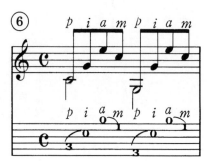

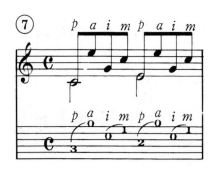

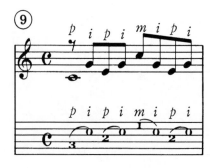

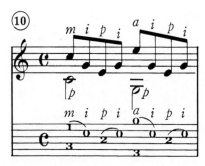
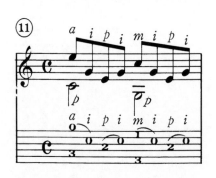
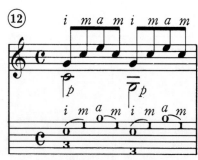

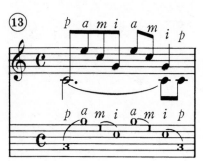

44

ARPEGGIOS AND ROLLS

$\frac{3}{4}$ and $\frac{6}{8}$

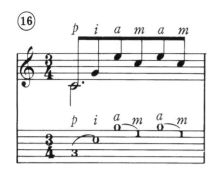

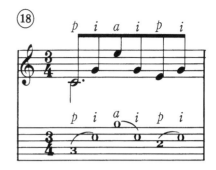

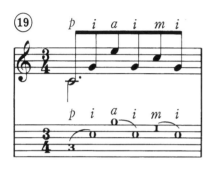

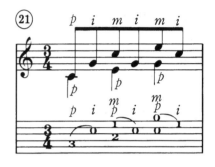

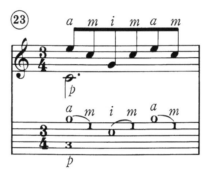

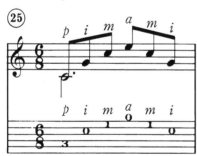

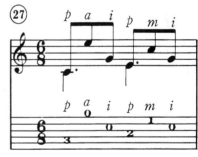

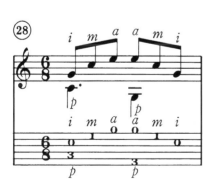

ARPEGGIOS AND ROLLS
Triplet Rhythm

In this section triplet rhythm means that there are three strums or plucks on every beat. The accent is on the first note or pluck in each group of three. It is a good idea to tap your foot on the beat or the oom.

Example

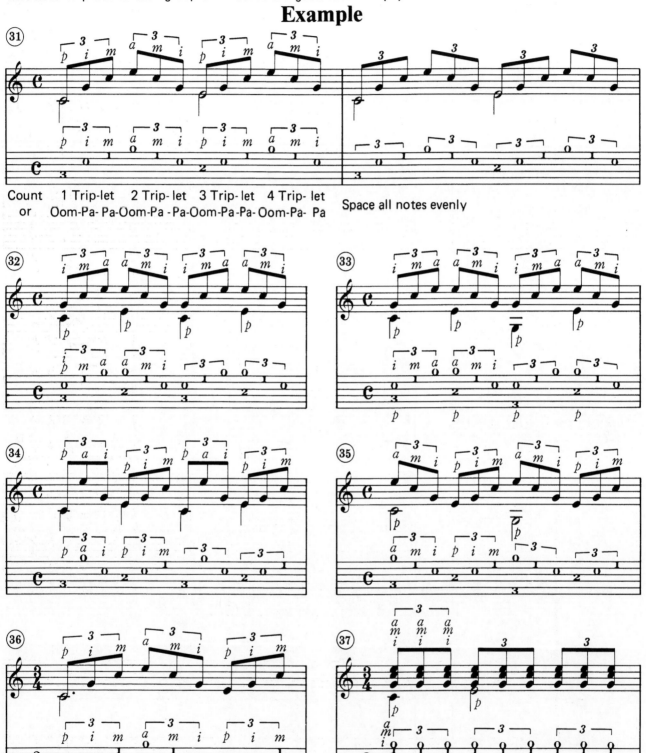

Count   1 Trip-let 2 Trip-let 3 Trip-let 4 Trip-let
or   Oom-Pa- Pa-Oom-Pa - Pa-Oom-Pa-Pa- Oom-Pa- Pa

Space all notes evenly

46

MORE LATIN ACCOMPANIMENT STYLES

Five Four Accompaniment

* Raise left hand slightly and release pressure on strings.

HOW TO TRANSPOSE FROM MALE TO FEMALE VOICE RANGE

Generally speaking, the female voice is a fifth higher than the male voice, or vice versa. In other words if a man sings a song in the key of C the girl probably would sing the same song in the key of G. However there are many exceptions to the rule. Refer to the circle of chords on page 15. Counterclockwise the chords move in fourths clockwise they move in fifths. From C to G is a fifth or G to D is a fifth. C to F is a fourth.

The following song is written in the key of C. When you have memorized the melody, try transposing it to the key of G. The new set of chords are written above the original chord symbols.

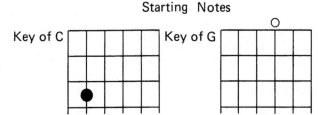

Starting Notes

MICHAEL, ROW THE BOAT ASHORE

2. Sister help me trim the sail,
   Hallelujah!
   Sister help me trim the sail,
   Hallelujah!

3. Jordan river is chilly and cold,
   Hallelujah!
   Chills the body but not the soul,
   Hallelujah!

4. Land of Canaan on the other side,
   Hallelujah!
   Land of Canaan on the other side,
   Hallelujah!

5. We are bound for the promised land,
   Hallelujah!
   We are bound for the promised land,
   Hallelujah!

WORRIED MAN BLUES

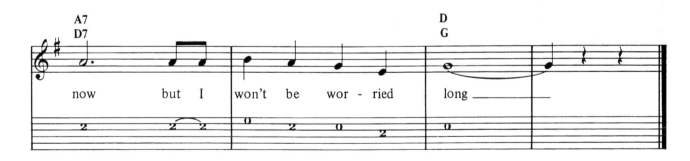

2. I went across the river, and lay   Repeat the first line two times.
   Me down to sleep
   When I woke up, had shackles on
   my feet.

THE CAPO
(Pronounced Kay-po)

The capo is an invaluable tool to the rhythm guitarist or singer guitarist. Not because the guitarist knowledge of the instrument is insufficient or because he is incapable of playing barre chords, (some of the world's greatest folk, country, and bluegrass guitarists use the capo) but simply because the beautiful ringing open chords are very desirable at times. This is especially true when they are played on the high third or high string tuning or the twelve string guitar.

Capos can be purchased at any music store and are either metal or elastic. The metal capo is stronger, but the elastic one is less likely to scratch the neck of your guitar.

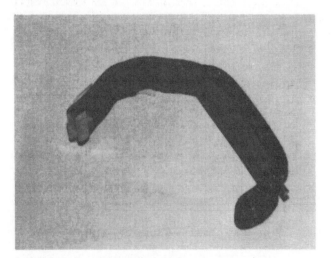

THE ELASTIC CAPO

THE ELASTIC CAPO ON THE GUITAR

THE METAL CAPO

THE METAL CAPO ON THE GUITAR

HOW TO USE THE CAPO

The distance between all the natural notes is a whole step (2 frets) except between B and C and E and F which are half steps (1 fret).

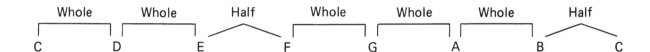

As an example, let us say you know a song in the key of C using C- F and G7 chords, but this is too low for you to sing comfortably so you want to transpose it to a higher key. Simply place the capo on the second fret and then sing the song using the same chord forms or fingering. C beocmes D, F becomes G and G7 becomes A7. You are now in the key of D. If you want to transpose the song even higher, place the capo on the fourth fret and use the same chords. Now you are in the key of E. C becomes E, F becomes A and G7 becomes B7. If you want to play in the key of F, then place the capo on the fifth fret. (Remember, it is only a half step or one fret from E to F.) Now C becomes F, F becomes Bb and G7 becomes C7.

The sharp (♯) raises a chord one half step or one fret. C♯ is one fret higher than C. If the capo is on the first fret, then C becomes C♯, F becomes F♯ and G7 becomes G♯7. If you place the capo on the sixth fret and play the same chords again, then you are in the key of F♯. (one fret higher than F.) C becomes F♯, F becomes B and G7 becomes C♯7.

The flat (b) lowers a chord one half step or one fret. To play in the key of Eb the capo should be on the third fret. Then C becomes Eb, F becomes Ab and G7 becomes Bb7. To play in the key of Db place the capo on the first fret. Then the same chord forms become Db, Gb and Ab7.

Any chord can be changed to a different key (or different name) by use of the capo.

A great deal of sheet music and many of the songs in "vocal with piano accompaniment" books are written in keys such as Bb, Eb and Ab which are usually rather difficult keys for the guitar. It is very easy to play in these keys and achieve the ringing open chord sound by use of the capo. For instance if a song is written in Eb and the chords are Eb, Ab, and Bb7, place the capo on the third fret and use the C, F and G7 forms. You are now playing in Eb.

If a song is written in a key that is too high or too low for your voice, move the capo up the fingerboard until you find a key that is comfortable for you.

Also, the capo can be helpful in transposing from the male voice range to the female voice range, or vice versa.

In the following section; if you are not familiar with the tune, play the meldoy without the capo and memorize it before playing the accompaniment.

Two Octave Chart

Steps

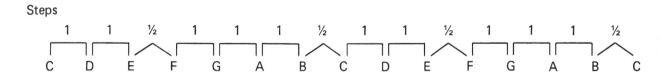

SHOO FLY

Capo on third fret Eb, Ab, Bb 7 use C, F, G7 forms.

See FUN WITH STRUMS FOR GUITAR for supplementary material.

THE FOGGY FOGGY DEW

English Folk song

Capo on third fret E♭, Fm A♭, B♭7 use Use C, Dm F, G7 forms.

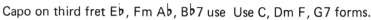

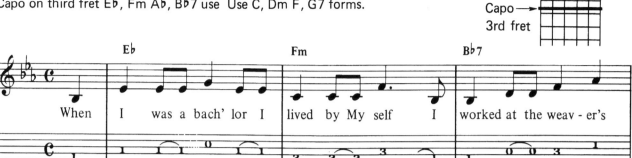

When I was a bach' lor I lived by My self I worked at the weav - er's

trade, and the on - ly on - ly thing I did that was wrong was to

woo a fair young maid I woo'd her in the win - ter time and

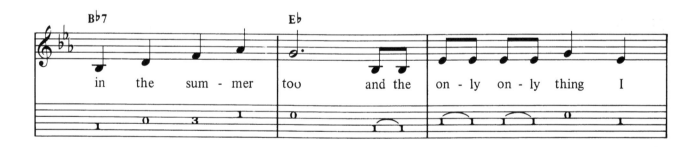

in the sum - mer too and the on - ly on - ly thing I

did that was wrong was to keep her from the fog - gy fog - gy dew

FRANKIE AND JOHNNY

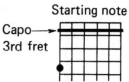

Capo on third fret Bb , Eb , F7 use G, C, D7

1. Fran - kie and John - ny were sweet hearts Law - dy Law - dy How they did
2. Fran - kie went down to the bar room or - dered a ____ bot - tle of

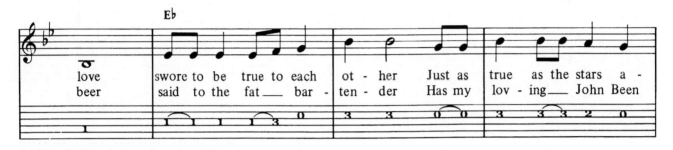

love swore to be true to each ot - her Just as true as the stars a -
beer said to the fat ____ bar - ten - der Has my lov - ing ____ John Been

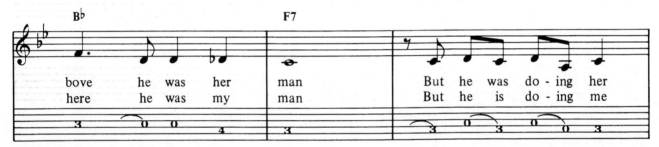

bove he was her man But he was do - ing her
here he was my man But he is do - ing me

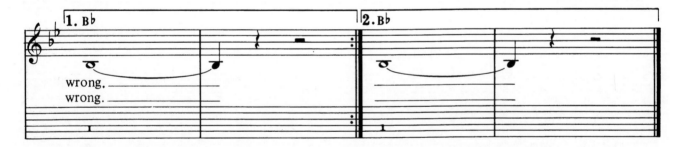

1. Bb wrong.
2. Bb wrong.

3. Well I aint gonna tell you no story
And I aint gonna tell you no lie
I saw your Johanny bout an hour ago
With a gal called Nellie Bly
He's your man etc.

4. Frankie went down to the corner
Looked up in a window so high
She saw her lovin' Johnny
A lovin' Nellie Bly
He was her man etc.

5. Frankie pulled out her pistol
I think it was a forty four
Root-a-toot-toot-four times she did shoot
And Johnny fell on the floor
He was her man etc.

6. Bring out your rubber tired buggy
Bring out your rubber tired hack
Gonna take little Johnny to
The grave yard, but he aint a-comming back,
He was her man, etc.

54

The following song is written in the key of D flat, a difficult key for some guitarists. However, this key is not too uncommon in piano-vocal books. It is a very simple matter to play accompaniment in this key by placing the capo on the first fret. Db, Gb and Ab7 become C, F and G7 Db+ becomes C+

CARELESS LOVE

Capo on The First Fret Db Gb Ab⁷ Use C F G7

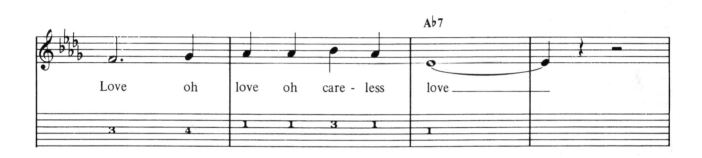

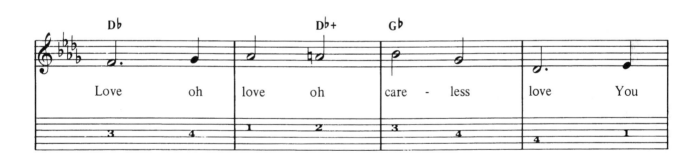

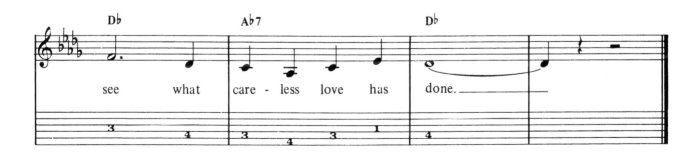

FINGER STYLE LEAD

This chapter will present a variety of finger style solos and exercises designed to raise the level of proficiency and improve the technique of the guitarist in prepration of the following chapters.

THE BLUES EVERY NIGHT

WHOLE NOTE BASSES

In the following solo the thumb will play whole notes on the bass strings. The index and middle fingers will be used to play the melody

Tommy Flint

To create a slight variation place the finger one or two frets lower on the first string and slide into the first note in measures 1, 3, 7 and 11.

The first and sixth strings are played simultaneously. The slide is very rapid

slide

B7

TWO BEAT BASS

In this style the thumb plays a steady two beat rhythm on the first and third beats. In this particular arrangement the thumb and middle finger play simultaneously on the counts of one and three. The index finger plays on two and four. Practice slowly at first.

HITTING ON TWO

Tommy Flint

CAISSONS
TWO BEAT

This is an excellent solo to practice in prepration for the thumb and finger picking chapter. The fourth finger is used on the first string second fret in A chord.

AROUND CAPE HORN
Two Beat Bass

Tommy Frint

This is an excellent solo to study in preparation for the steady bass or thump bass rhythm. In the last eight measures the third finger is used to play the alternate bass on the sixth string. (left hand)

RIGHT HAND EXERCISES

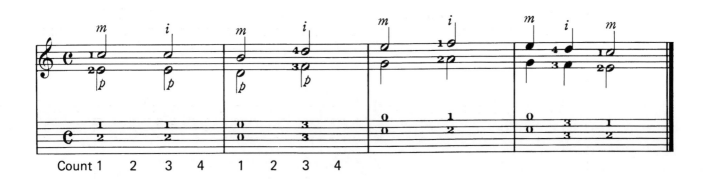

Count 1   2   3   4   1   2   3   4

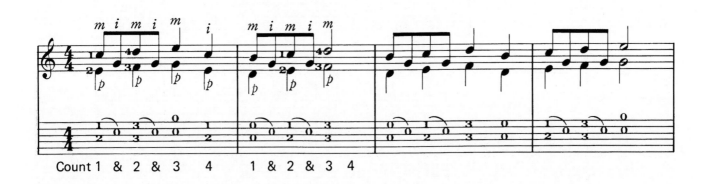

Count 1 & 2 & 3   4   1 & 2 & 3   4

60

FRERE JACQUES

POP GOES THE WEASEL

Remember: How to count $\frac{6}{8}$ time? See page 38 (in accompaniment section.) There are six counts in each measure. The eighth note (♪) receives one count. The quarter note (♩) receives two beats and the dotted note (♩.) receives three beats. All count are spaced evenly.

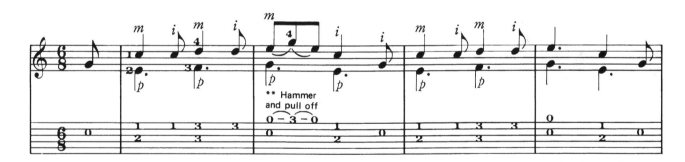

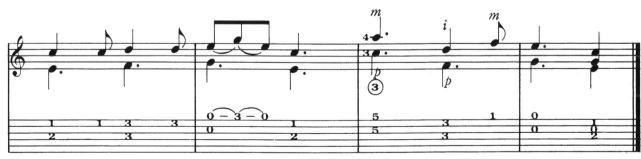

**Pluck the open string. While it is still ringing hammer (press down abruptly) the 4th finger on the third fret. Then pull the finger off allowing the open string to sound again.

*The C note is on the third string, fifth fret.

A SUNDAY STROLL

Tommy Flint

The following solo employs the strolling bass rhythm. The thumb plays on the first second and third beats.

THE WALTZ STYLE

The thumb and middle finger play simultaneously on the first beat. The thumb and index finger play the rhythm strokes on the second and third beats.

EASY COUNTRY WALTZ

Tommy Flint

A COUNTRY MORNING WALTZ

The middle and index fingers are used to play the eighth notes. Alternate picking is used.

Tommy Flint

NEW CHORDS

A

Fm — Can be used

The remainder of the chords are the same as used on previous pages.

ARKANSAS TRAVELER

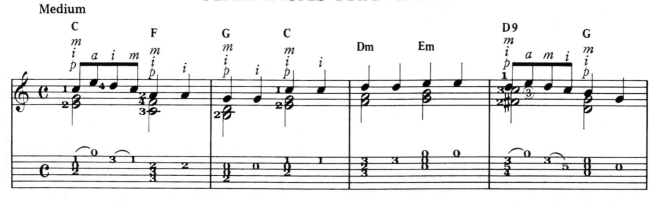

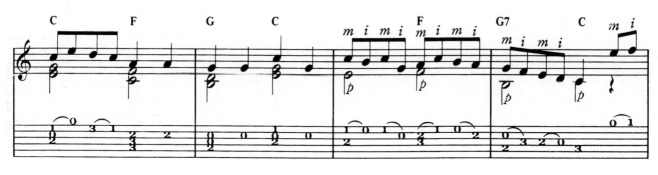

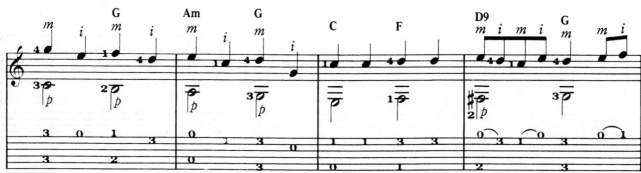

This solo should be practiced slowly at first. As coordination and control are developed the speed should gradually be increased until a moderate tempo has been reached.

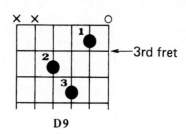

D9

used in measure number four.

AURA LEE

THUMB AND FINGER PICKING

Various terms have been used to describe this style such as "Thumb Style" "Finger Style" "Thump Bass" "Claw Hammer""and" "Hog Wallow Pickin" to name a few; but, probably the most commonly used term today is "Travis Pickin." This term is used to indicate a wide variety of finger picking styles from the early southern blues pickers to the modern "City folk guitarist", including all of the styles that have been developed by the Merle Travis and Chet Atkins influenced people between the two extremes. At this time the term obviously does not necessarily apply directly to Merle Travis or his great and very distinctive style.

Merle has said that he was inspired by two coal miners named Mose Rager and Ike Everly, who had streamlined the finger style and developed it to a very high degree of proficiency. They had no doubt been inspired by the black blues and ragtime guitarists who had migrated to the west Kentucky coal fields to work in the mines. I remember hearing the names Amos Johnson and Jim Mason as two of the men who contributed to the evolution of the finger style guitar. Some of these men had probably come from the deep south and south-west and brought the blues from the cotton fields and plantations. (Mose was one of the best blues singers and players I have ever heard and some of Merle's great blues have become classics.) Some of them had possibly come by way of the Mississippi Valley and picked up the styles of the Ragtime Pianist who were working in the area. So this style is probably the result of many infuences and roots: Blues, Ragtime, Dixieland, Etc.

The thumb and finger style is actually two parts played simultanesouly on one guitar. The thumb plays rhythm on the bass strings and lower part of the chord while the index finger plays the melody or syncopated improvisation on the treble strings and upper part of the chord. The bass strings are muffled by the heel of the hand.

Merle has been an insiration to many guitarists. One is the great Chet Atkins, the guitar genius who has been an inspiration to hundreds of guitarists.

During the fifties and sixties another style of finger picking was introduced by the "Modern" or "City folk-musicians." This method of picking was closer to the bluegrass banjo style and did not always employ the steady bass rhythm as the Travis style does. However this was called "Travis Picking" by many people. In recent years "Travis Picking" has become the term used to cover almost all finger styles other than basic accompaniment.

This section, will attempt to give some insight into many of these styles beginning with the basic thumb and finger style.

In addition to Mose Rager, Ike Everly, Merle Travis, and Chet Atkins, there are many other fine musicians who have contributed to the finger style guitar. To name a few: the fine guitarist and composer James "Spider" Rich, Joe Edwards, Paul Yandell, Jerry Reed, Lenny Breau, Odell Martin, Ralph Martin Bill Carver and many whose names I have heard mentioned but have not had the honor of meeting such as Lester English, Johnny Hammer, and George Mauzy;

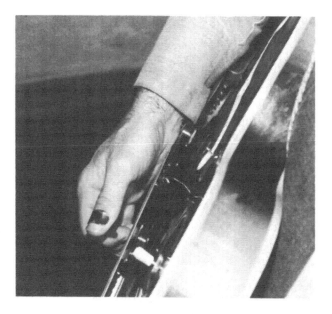

| HOW TO MUFFLE THE BASS STRINGS | THE RIGHT HAND POSITION |

In the first section of this chapter, the thumb and index finger will be used most of the time. The other three fingers may rest on the guard plate. However I would suggest resting only the fourth finger, as this will facilitate the change to using two and three fingers.

MUFFLE THE BASS STRINGS

The heel of the right hand should muffle the three bass strings near the bridge in order to produce a muted, solid thump tone. Don't touch the strings too far away from the bridge or you will get a dead thud. If you touch them too close to the bridge, they will ring too much. If will take a bit of practice and experimentation to find the right sound.

HOW TO PLAY RHYTHM WITH THE THUMB

Hold C chord.

Slowly and evenly count 1-2-3-4 or say Oom-Pah-Oom-Pah.

On 1 and 3 or the Ooms pick the fifth string.

On the counts of 2 and 4 or the Pahs pick the fourth and third strings simultaneously. When the melody is on the third string the thumb will pick only the fourth string on the Pahs.

Now try changing from C to G7 chords while keeping a steady Oom-Pah-Oom-Pah rhythm.

	C				G7			
Count or	1 Oom	2 Pah	3 Oom	4 Pah	1 Oom	2 Pah	3 Oom	4 Pah
Strings	⑤	③④	⑤	③④	⑤	③④	⑤	③④

This rhythm should be practiced until it becomes automatic, or is practically a reflex. The thumb should be capable of holding a steady rhythm no matter what the fingers are doing.

IMPORTANT

If it is too difficult to play both the fourth and third strings on the Pahs then pick the fourth string only. It is far more important at this time to develop a feel for the style and to be able to "Keep Time" or hold a steady, even rhythm.

Played

Use the thumb only

THE BASIC THUMB RHYTHM

To avoid cluttering the tablature with a seeming myriad of numerals and to facilitate the reading of the chart, the basic thumb rhythm will be written as follows. The thumb will still play both the fourth and third strings on the pahs, or the counts of two and four.

Written

Use the thumb only

If picking both the fourth and third strings on the Pahs proves to be too difficult at this time, it might be a good idea to play only the fourth string as written until you develop a bit more skill and control.

ALTERNATE BASSES

Alternate bass notes on the first and third beats or the "Ooms" will add a great deal of flavor and a feeling to the rhythm. To play alternate bass notes on B7 chord move the second finger of the left hand only, on the third beat. See chord chart on page **20** in accompaniment section.

Use thumb only

REMEMBER! If playing two strings on the "Pahs" is too difficult, then play the fourth string only.

BASIC THUMB RHYTHM USING ALTERNATE BASSES

See alternate bass chart on page 20 in accompaniment section.

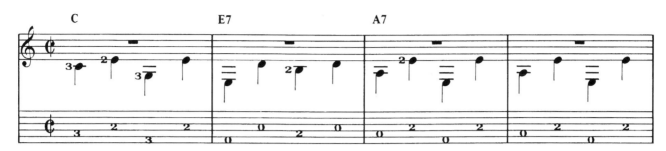

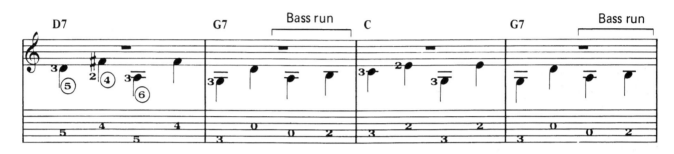

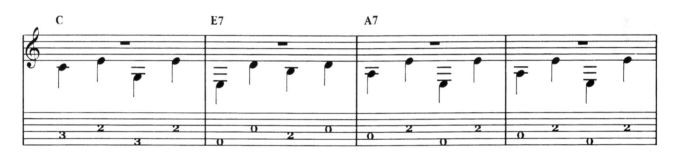

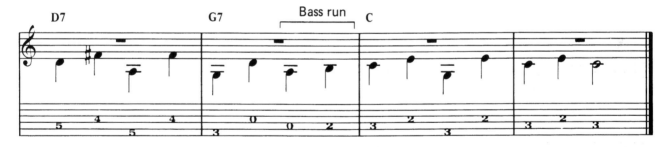

■ = Root note
▲ = Alternate bass

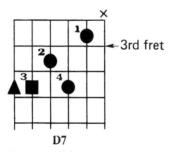

D7
Used on this page.

IMPORTANT

If it is too difficult playing both the fourth and third strings on the "Pahs", then pick the fourth string only. It is far more important at this time to develop a "Feel" for the style and to be able to "Keep time" or hold a steady even rhythm with the thumb. Remember the thumb must keep time no matter what the fingers are doing.

In the following example only C and G7 chords are used. The thumb should play a steady, muffled, alternate bass note rhythm. The index finger should be used to play the melody note on the first beat or first Oom in each of the first eight measures. In the last eight measures the index finger should play on the first and third beats or both Ooms.

Have patience and keep on practicing until you have mastered this exercise and you will have won the battle. From now on every new tune should come a bit easier.

ONE — THREE

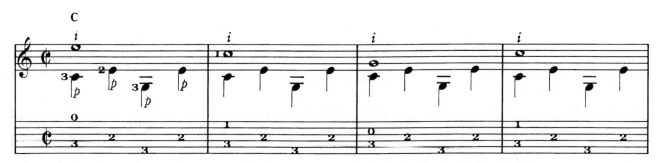

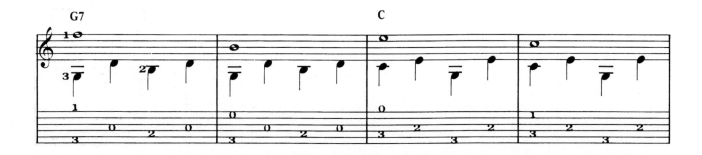

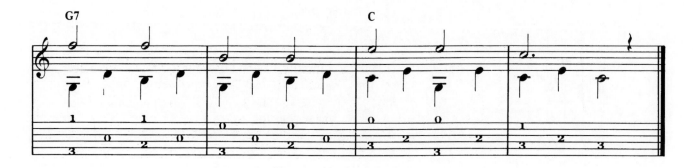

In the third and eleventh measures of the following solo, use the fourth finger on the first string, third fret.

Be sure to keep the steady muffled Oom Pah rhythm with the thumb.

In measures number 2 6 9 10 13 and 14 the melody notes are on the first third and fourth beats, or Oom-Oom-Pah.

THE OOM PAH THUMP

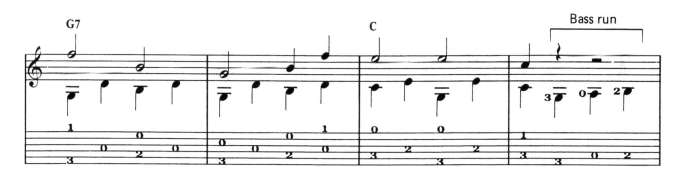

73

ADDING NOTES TO THE CHORDS

Due to the fact that some melodies are based on the scale as well as the chordal tones, it sometimes becomes necessary to add tones to the chords in order to play the melody. As an example, the first, second and third strings at the third fret and the open second string may be added to C chord. Also the the first string at the first fret can be used. When playing G7 chord, the second string at the first and third frets can be used and the first string can be played open or at the third fret. Added notes can do a great deal to enhance an arrangement and will be used frequently in this style.

GO TELL AUNT RHODY
(The Old Grey Goose Is Dead)

74

THUMB AND TWO FINGER PICKING

Generally speaking, the index and middle fingers will play alternate strokes on the melody line. However, in some instances this may prove impractical so it is really a matter to be left to the good judgement of the individual performer. When a passage of three or more eighth notes are played in a row, it becomes necessary to use alternate picking. It is hoped that the following examples will give some insight into the thumb and two finger style.

GOODNIGHT LADIES

LITTLE BROWN JUG

RED RIVER VALLEY

SYNCOPATION

A very colorful and outstanding ingredient of this style is the flowing, spontaneous feel of the melody above the steady muffled bass rhythm. This is achieved by syncopation. The definition of syncopation is irregularity of rhythm or placing the accents on beats which are usually unaccented. In this section syncopation means that the melody notes are played between the rhythm beats of the thumb.

In example number one the finger plays on the "and" after the first, second, and third beats. In actuality this is a type of alternate picking, the thumb and finger alternating from rhythm to melody. I have heard banjo players call this method "Double Thumbing." I would suggest using the two finger and thumb method. However it is possible to play this exercise using the index finger and thumb only.

The following exercise is a two measure pattern. The easiest way to count the two measures is "Boom-Chick-A-Boom-a-Chick-Boom-a-chick-a-Boom-Chick. Again it is possible to use the index finger only, however we suggest the two finger picking.

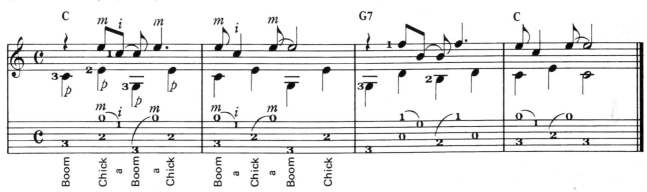

The count is the same in this pattern as in the preceeding exercise. Nevertheless, it is imperative that you use the thumb and two finger style because there are more than two consecutive eighth notes in the melody line.

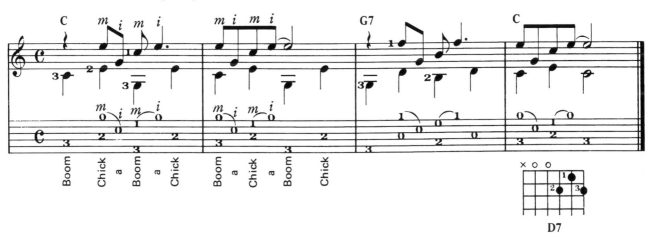

BLUE MOUNTAIN TRAIN

TWO FINGER SYNCOPATED MELODY

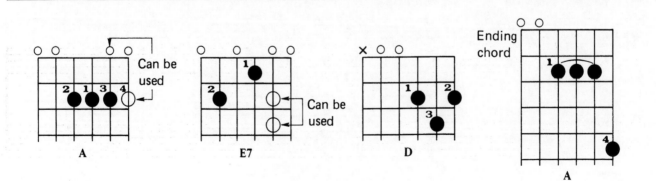

I'VE BEEN WORKING ON THE RAILROAD

TWO FINGER AND THUMB RECOMMENDED

The chords used in "I've Been Working On The Railroad."

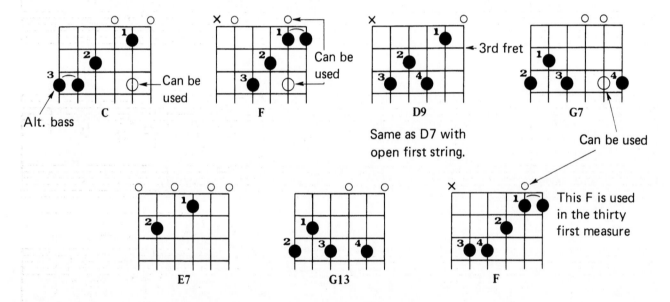

C — Alt. bass — Can be used

F — Can be used

D9 — 3rd fret — Same as D7 with open first string.

G7 — Can be used

E7

G13

F — Can be used — This F is used in the thirty first measure

* In measure number fifteen the fourth finger is on the second string. (G7) In measure number sixteen the fourth finger is moved to the first string and the second string is played open.

The Chords Used in "JOHN HENRY"

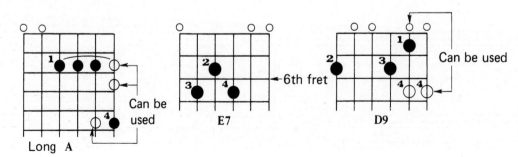

Long A — Can be used

E7 — 6th fret

D9 — Can be used

JOHN HENRY

The ♪ sign above or below a note means to release the pressure of the left hand on the strings to deaden the sound. Don't take the fingers off the strings. Just raise them slightly.

* If you are not familiar with the "hammer" and "pull off" see "Authentic Bruegrass Guitar" published by Mel Bay.

TWO STRING HARMONY

We are still working with a two finger and thumb method. However, in this style the fingers (usually the index and middle) will pick two strings simultaneously.

THE MARINES' HYMN

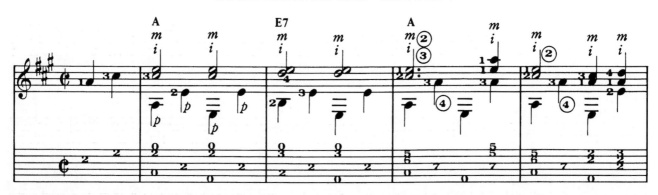

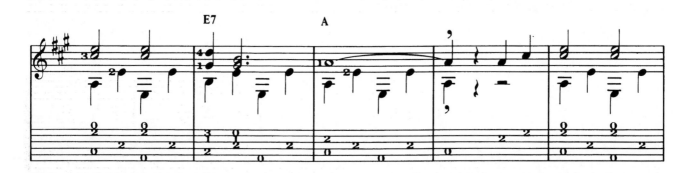

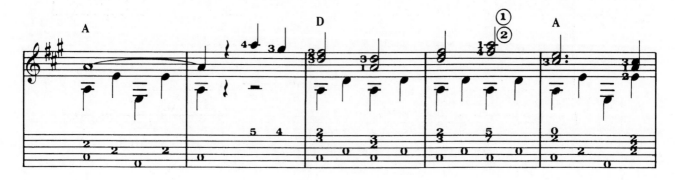

How to play measures number four, twelve, and twenty eight: the first half of the measure is "A" chord in the fifth position. (fret). The last half is "A" in the second position.

In measure number thirty one, the melody and harmoy notes are on the first and third strings using the middle and index fingers (*m* and *i*)

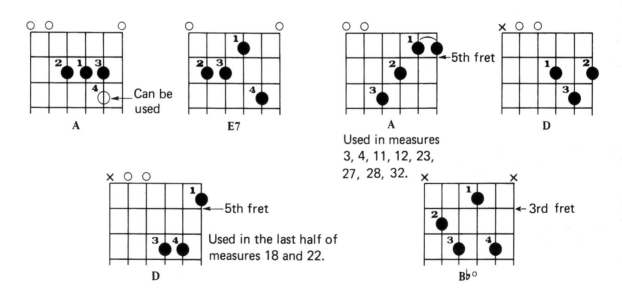

A

E7

A

Used in measures
3, 4, 11, 12, 23,
27, 28, 32.

D

D — Used in the last half of measures 18 and 22.

Bb°

SOME THOUGHTS ON CHORDS

As this is primarily a chord style, it is essential that you learn as many chords and chord inversions as possible. These should include some barre chords, chords using the thumb, movable and open string forms. It would be impossible to memorize all chord forms, as learning chords is a never ending process. We feel it would be wise at this point to purchase a good book on chord building. If you understand how the notes are put together to construct the chord, it becomes much easier to find the appropriate form for the particular task at hand.

The chords shown in this section are some of the most commonly used forms and will be used with others throughout the remainder of this book. This section may be used for easy reference.

Movable Chord Forms

There are two common fingerings for this chord, both of which are shown below. In both cases the index finger should bar all six strings.

It is not necessary to hold both the ⑤ and ⑥ string together. The third finger can move back and fourth to play the alternate bass notes.

The fifth string is not part of this chord. The thumb should skip over this string when playing the bass notes.

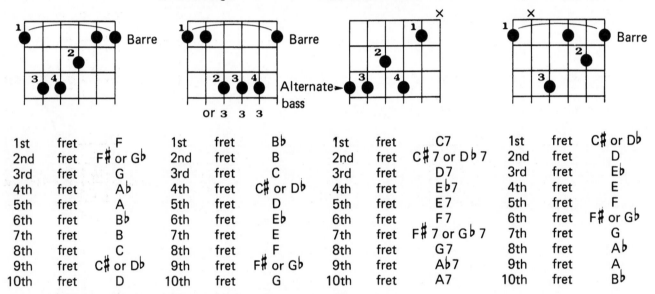

1st fret	F		1st fret	Bb		1st fret	C7		1st fret	C# or Db
2nd fret	F# or Gb		2nd fret	B		2nd fret	C#7 or Db7		2nd fret	D
3rd fret	G		3rd fret	C		3rd fret	D7		3rd fret	Eb
4th fret	Ab		4th fret	C# or Db		4th fret	Eb7		4th fret	E
5th fret	A		5th fret	D		5th fret	E7		5th fret	F
6th fret	Bb		6th fret	Eb		6th fret	F7		6th fret	F# or Gb
7th fret	B		7th fret	E		7th fret	F#7 or Gb7		7th fret	G
8th fret	C		8th fret	F		8th fret	G7		8th fret	Ab
9th fret	C# or Db		9th fret	F# or Gb		9th fret	Ab7		9th fret	A
10th fret	D		10th fret	G		10th fret	A7		10th fret	Bb

THE SAME CHORDS USING THE THUMB.

These chords are rather difficult and should not be attempted until you have attained some degree of proficiency in playing the standard chords.

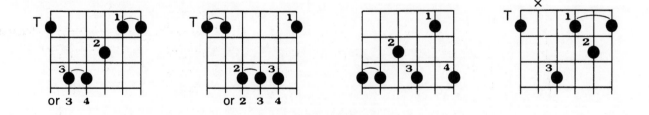

See Mel Bay's Deluxe Guitar Chords and Rhythm Chord System.

84

MOVABLE CHORD FORMS

Barre chords

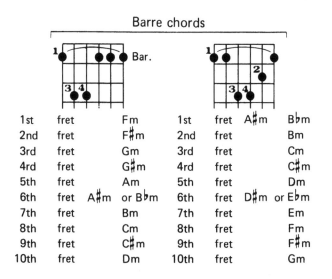

The Same chords using thumb.

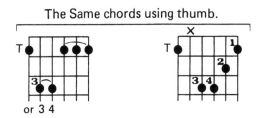

This set of chords has the same names as the set at the left. Only the fingering is different.

fret			fret		
1st		Fm	1st	A♯m	B♭m
2nd		F♯m	2nd		Bm
3rd		Gm	3rd		Cm
4rd		G♯m	4rd		C♯m
5th		Am	5th		Dm
6th	A♯m or B♭m		6th	D♯m or E♭m	
7th		Bm	7th		Em
8th		Cm	8th		Fm
9th		C♯m	9th		F♯m
10th		Dm	10th		Gm

Upper Position Open String Chords

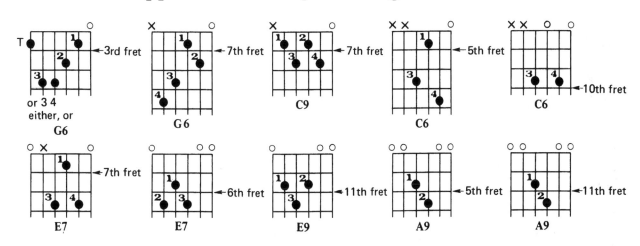

More Open String Chords

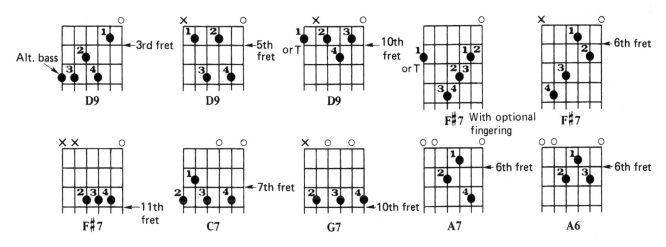

See the MERLE TRAVIS GUITAR STYLE by Merle Travis and Tommy Flint
Mel Bay Publications MB 93344

UPPER POSITION OPEN STRING CHORD STYLE

This style has a sustained, legato quality as opposed to the crisp somewhat staccato feel of the original thumb style. The right hand rhythm is exactly the same, a steady muffled bass.

The open string inversions may be slightly confusing at first because some of the strings which would normally sound higher will sound lower and vice versa. I believe that mastery of the chords will suggest numerous possibilities and means of expression.

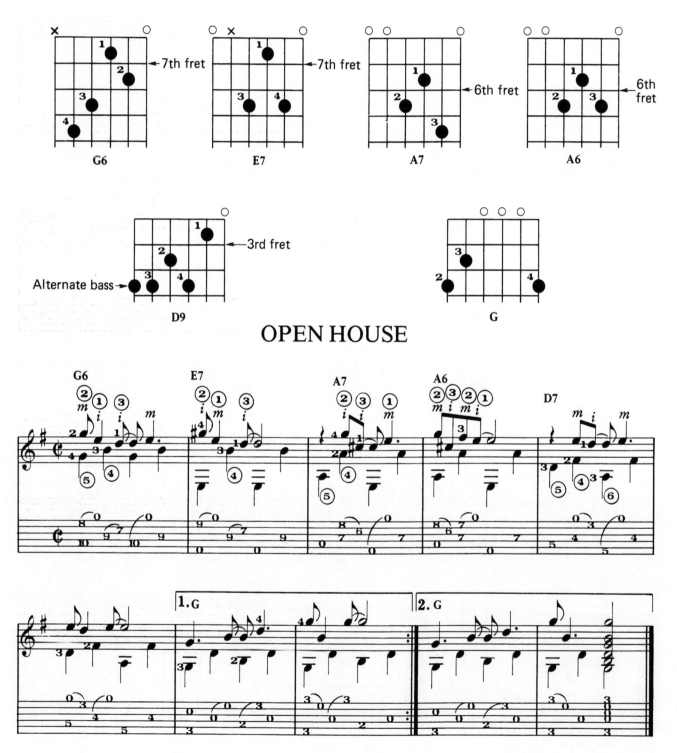

OPEN HOUSE

JESSE JAMES

This is the first solo to utilize the six string barre chord which is the B7 in measures number fourteen and thirty. We are also using the two and three string harmony in measures sixteen and seventeen.

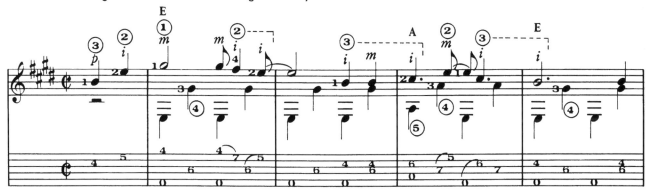

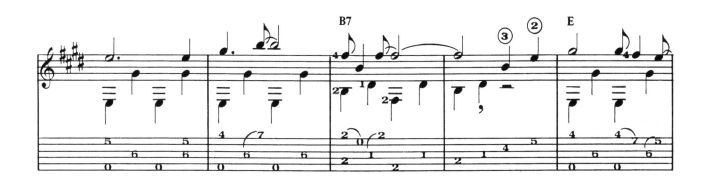

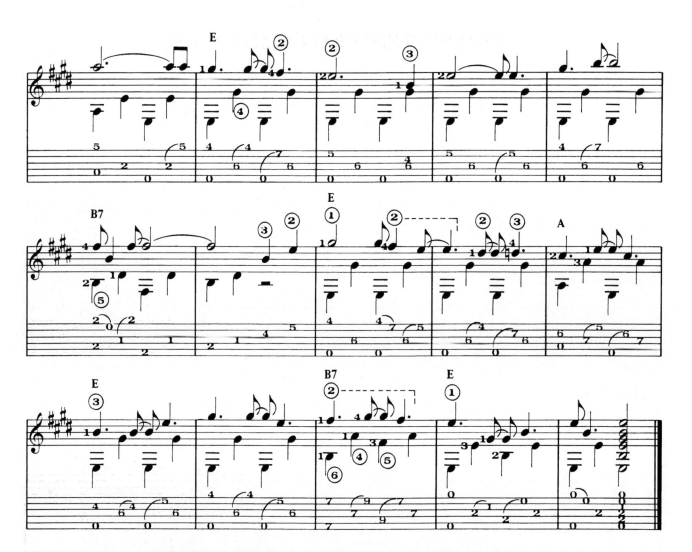

THE CHORDS USED IN THIS SOLO

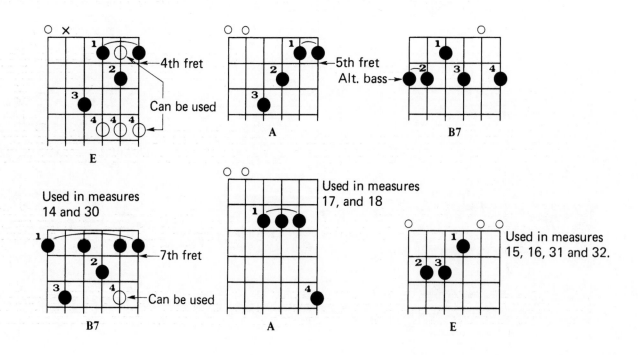

4th fret

Can be used

E

5th fret

A

Alt. bass→

B7

Used in measures
14 and 30

7th fret

Can be used

B7

Used in measures
17, and 18

A

Used in measures
15, 16, 31 and 32.

E

STRING BENDING ON CHORDS

String bending on chords is a very colorful ingredient of finger style guitar when used in good state. This is quite different than bending the single strings, which will be discussed in a later chapter. To bend the string while playing the chord, the thumb should continue the rhythm on the bass strings. The fourth finger will be used to bend the first or second string to somewhere between a quarter and half tone.

The bend is executed by using the fourth finger to push the string in an upward motion. In the example below the bend should begin on the second beat and gradually extend over the third and fourth beats reaching the highest tone on the fourth. The tone should graduate from the natural tone of the eilght fret (C) to slightly below the tone of the ninth fret (C♯), somewhat less than a half note.

The bend will be indicated by a curved line over the note ⌣.

The fingers should be raised enough to deaden the strings when indicated by by the sign (❜).

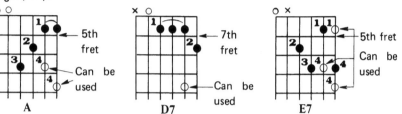

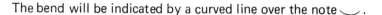

DRAKESBORO COAL DRAG

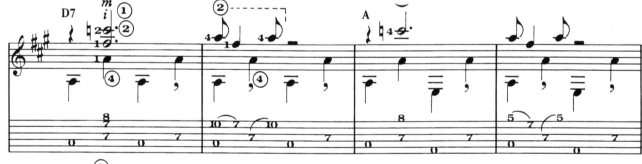

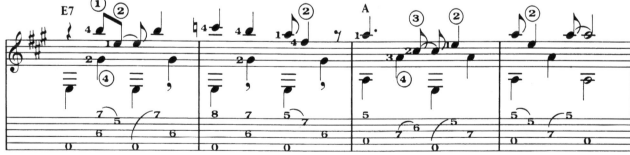

ROLLS

The "roll" is a group of notes, usually the notes of a chord played consecutively in a pattern. The notes should be spaced evenly in a straight eighth note rhythm. The steady bass rhythm of the thumb will be discontinued for the duration of the roll.

Although the roll is played with a straight eighth note feel, the strings are picked consecutively in groups of three, so consequently the roll has a syncopated feel.

Example

The following example is written in one part to facilitate the reading. Also the three note grouping is indicated. The basic roll below is written correctly in two parts although the picking is identical.

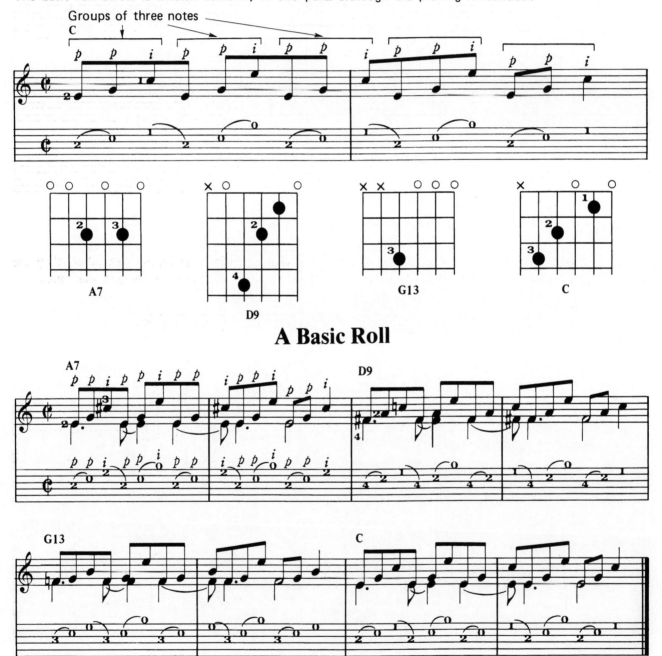

A Basic Roll

A TWO FINGER ROLL

The following roll employs the thumb, index and middle fingers.

The chords are the same as one the previous page.

REMEMBER!

When written in two parts, the rolls appear to be rather complex and formidable; but remember, they are picked simply as straight eighth notes. Just hold the chords with the left hand and sustain the tones.

THE TWO FINGER BACKWARD ROLL

This is just the opposite of the preceding roll.

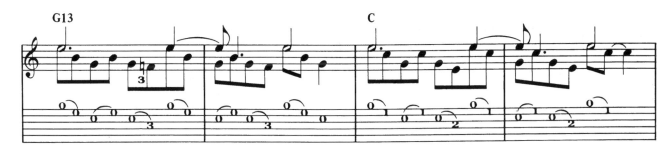

ROLLING SOUTH
A Two Finger Roll

Tommy Flint

THE THUMB AND THREE FINGER ROLL

The three finger roll was shown in the accompaniment section as a background pattern. However, it can be used occasionally in playing lead, or melody. It is especially effective when used for introductions.

Example

See chords on page 14. Practice slowly at first, gradually increasing the tempo with each practice session until a fairly bright speed has been achieved.

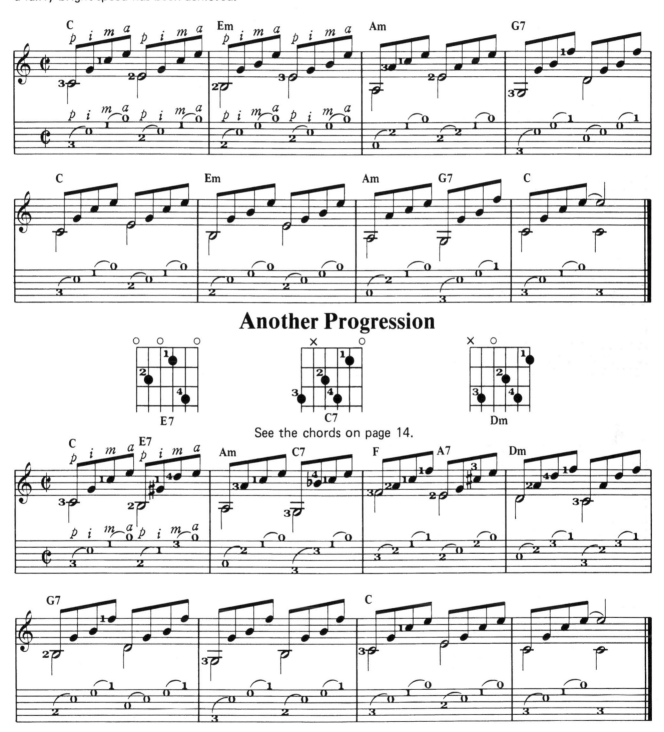

Another Progression

See the chords on page 14.

93

ROLLING DOWN THE CUMBERLAND

THREE FINGER ROLL

This pattern is used occasionally behind fast or bright tempo narrations or "Talking Songs".

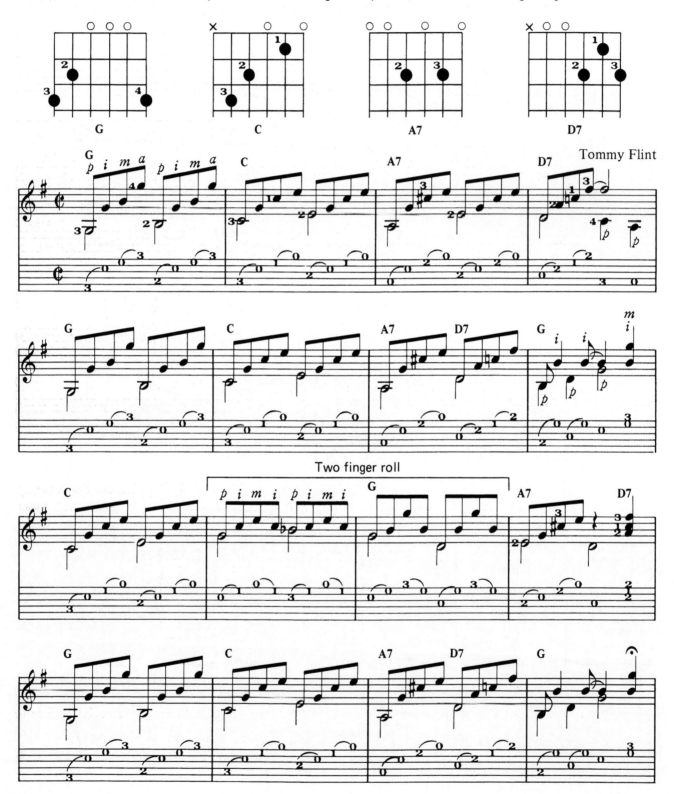

THE COMPANY STORE BOOGIE

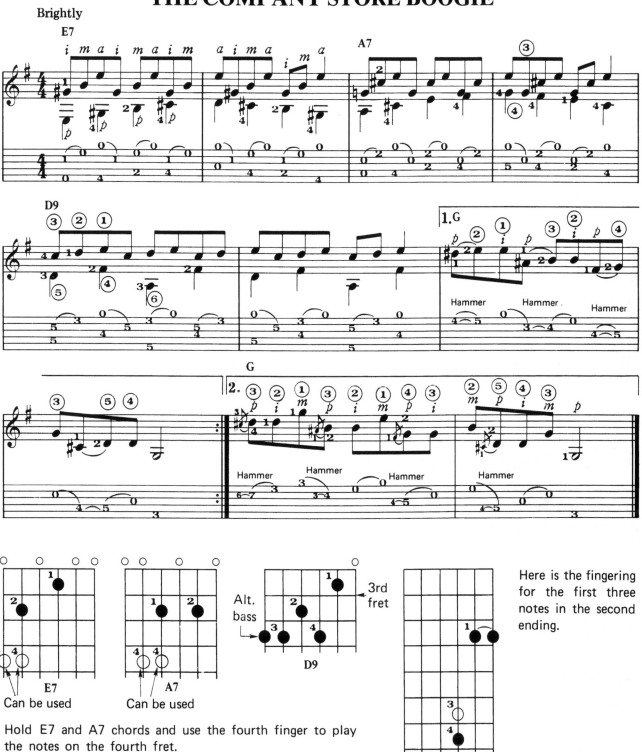

Here is the fingering for the first three notes in the second ending.

Hold E7 and A7 chords and use the fourth finger to play the notes on the fourth fret.

This solo is a three finger roll with a walking bass through the first four measures. In the fifth and sixth measures the three finger roll is still used, but with an alternate bass.

The first ending is a "Hammer On" to open string. The second ending is a two finger roll with a slur on the first note in each group. Both endings should be played as smoothly as possible.

In the first two measures of the following solo the index finger plays a harmony line on the third string while the middle finger is playing the melody on the first and second strings. The thumb should play the steady muffled bass rhythm. However, the bass notes on the first and third beats move down in half steps to form a counter melody. This pattern is repeated in the ninth — tenth and twenty fifth — twenty sixth measures. The F chord is anticipated in the fifteenth measure. Also the chords in measures thirty and thirty one.

MY OLD KENTUCKY HOME

96

Finger style guitar has been used extensively in gospel music and is quite appropriate in most cases.

PRECIOUS MEMORIES

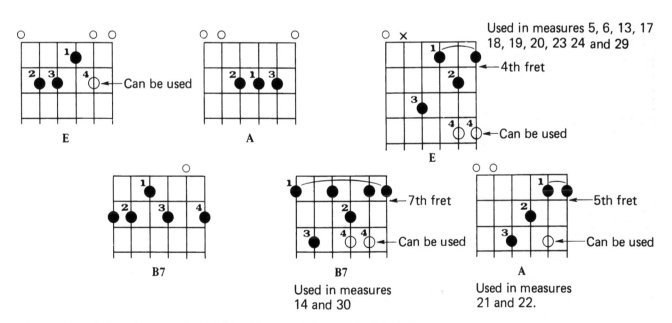

The chords used in Precious memories

Used in measures 5, 6, 13, 17
18, 19, 20, 23 24 and 29

← Can be used

← 4th fret

E

A

← Can be used

E

B7

Used in measures
14 and 30

Used in measures
21 and 22.

See Mel Bay's "GOSPEL GUITAR" by Tommy Flint and Neil Griffin

FANNIE LOU

Moderately slow

Tommy Flint

OLD JOE CLARK

Hoe down with a steady bass

THE FLOP EARED MULE
Hoedown

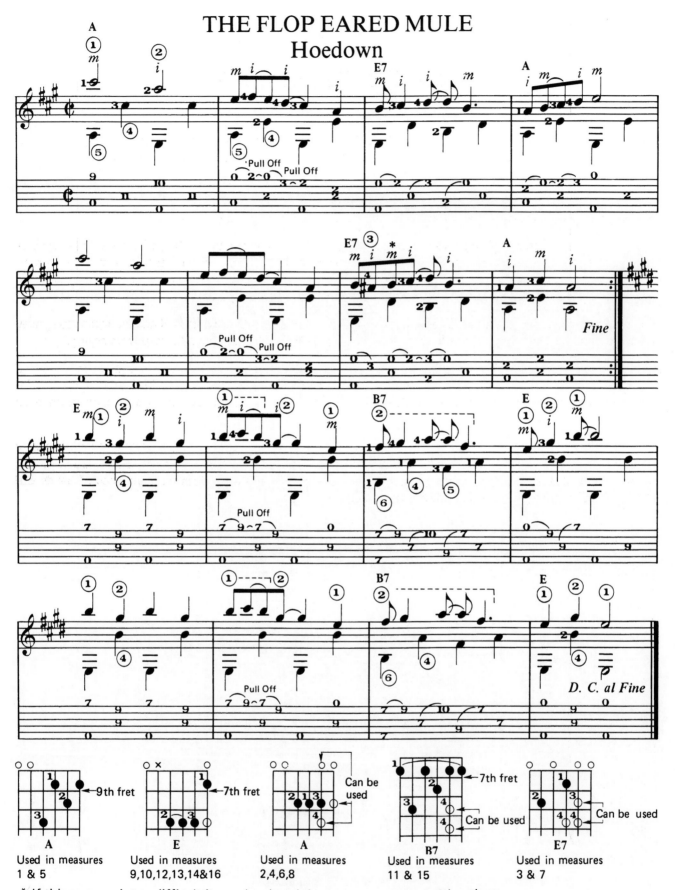

* If this measure is too difficult it may be played the same as measure number three.

FINGER STYLE BLUES

This is not intended to be a history of the blues. The intent is merely to show the styles of some of the great finger style blues guitarists and hopefully kindle a spark of interest and creativity in the student.

The term "Blues" is a semantic problem which we will leave to the linguistic experts and musicologist to ponder. However, generally speaking, "Authentic Country Blues" could probably be defined as an emotional state of loneliness, sorrow, despair or unrequited love expressed through the music.

An essential requirement of the blues guitarist is the ability to convey the feeling of the music, — song or instrumental, — to the listener, or in other words, establish the proper mental attitude. Although he may not have experienced the exact happening as sung or played about in the tune, you can be sure he has paid his dues in life, as this is another requirement of becoming a master blues guitarist.

Paradoxically however, not all blues are sad or mournful. Some are rather whimsical and are meant to convey a feeling of humor. In other words to laugh at misfortune, as in the cliche "Laugh to keep from crying."

While technique is not the main concern of the blues guitarist, it is a very, very important factor in his overall make up. The greater the technique of the guitarist, the better able he is to express himself through the instrument. Technique and control are very desirable attributes so long as the music does not become mechanical and does come from the heart or soul.

Although there are various blues styles from different sections of the country, finger style blues are basically thump bass rhythms played with the thumb while the finger or fingers play the melody on the treble strings or _____ single string melody interspersed with chords and laced with an abundance of bends and slides. The thump rhythm can be either alternate or drone bass.

While this is by no means meant to be a book on theory, a bit of knowledge of the blues scale, progressions and rhythms will be helpful at this time.

THE BLUES PROGRESSION

The most commonly used sequence of chords is the twelve measure pattern known as the "Blues Progression." This progression is divided into three lines or sections. The words and melody of the first line are usually repeated in the second line. (Due to the blue notes, which will be shown later, the melody will usually harmonize with either the I or IV chord.) The last line is usually different in both words and music However in some cases the melody is the same in all three sections. I would guess that at least ninety eight per cent of the blues are based on this twelve measure progression.

If you are not familiar with the I (tonic), IV (sub dominant) and V (dominant) chords please refer to page 15 in the accompaniment section of this book. The V is a seventh chord. The I and IV chords can be either major or seventh when playing the blues. Sometimes seventh or ninth chords sound good for all three changes.

THE BASIC PROGRESSION

words   Saw you last night baby in a telephone booth

    I   I   I   I

    Saw you last night baby in a telephone booth

    IV   IV   I   I

    Asked you'bout it honey   you wouldnt tell the   truth

    V   V   I   I

VARIATION NUMBER 1.

In this progression the IV chord is substituted in measure number two.

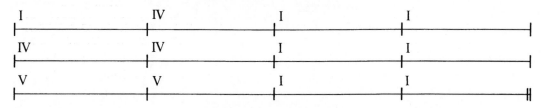

I	IV	I	I
IV	IV	I	I
V	V	I	I

VARIATION NUMBER 2.

In this progression the IV chord is substituted in measure number ten.

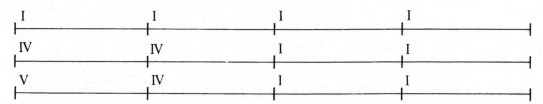

I	I	I	I
IV	IV	I	I
V	IV	I	I

Note. The IV chord can be substituted in both the second and tenth measures or the second, ninth and tenth. This is entirely a matter of personal judgement and good taste.

BLUES RHYTHM

Most blues are in $\frac{4}{4}$, C or ¢ time. (See page 13 in accompaniment section.) Most blues are also played with either a triplet rhythm feel or shuffle rhythm.

Triplets

In triplet rhythm three strokes are played on each count. All of the strokes are spaced evenly.

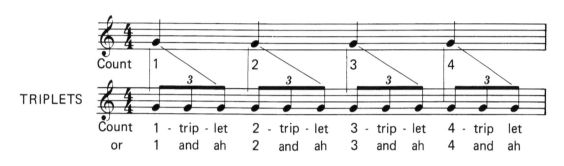

Shuffle

Shuffle rhythm is played the same as triplets with the middle note omitted.

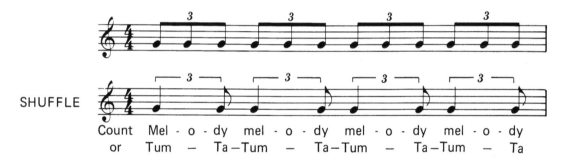

In order to facilitate reading, the shuffle rhythm will be written as follows.

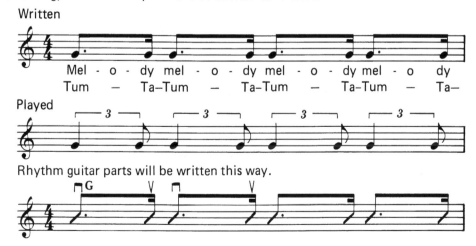

Rhythm guitar parts will be written this way.

THE SCALE USED FOR MOST COUNTRY BLUES

The seventh and third notes are flatted (of major scale). The natural fifth and the flatted fifth are both used and the second is omitted. However any note may be flatted or sharped if this seems desirable to the player.

The Open String Scale (Key Of E)

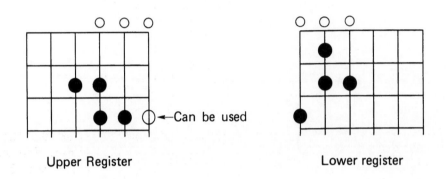

Upper Register   Lower register

The Two Octave Scale

This two octave scale should be practiced until committed to memory. This is not as difficult as it may sound, as the scale is very pleasing to the ear. Suprisingly this scale may be used with either the I or the IV chord as it harmonizes well with either chord. For example in the key of E this scale can be used with either E or A chords. In many instances it sounds very well with the V chord (B7), but in any event, good taste should be ex-exercised.

The Movable Scale

The movable scale is shown on the following page. There are no open strings in this scale, so it is possible to play in any key by moving up or down the fingerboard. The first finger on the first string determines the key. (See chart on next page.) For instance, if the first finger is on the the third fret you are in the key of G. If the first finger is on the fifth fret, you are in the key of A etc. Remember the scale can be used with both the I and the IV chord.

THE TWO OCTAVE SCALE

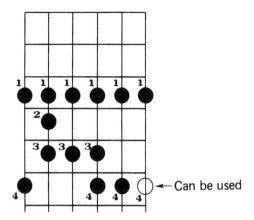

← Can be used

This scale can be played in any key by moving higher or lower on the fingerboard. The first finger determines the key. If the first finger is on the fifth fret you are in the key of A etc.

FIRST STRING
NOTES TO THE TWELFTH FRET

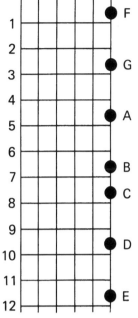

Only the natural notes are shown. The sharp is one fret higher and the flat is one fret lower. (see page 84.)

BLUES PROGRESSION

Demonstrating how scale will harmonize with the three chords.

TWO TO GO

The next three solos are easy arrangements written in the two beat and stroll rhythms so that you may become accustomed to the blues and learn to "feel" or anticipate the chord changes. All exercises, solos etc. should be practiced until they seem natural and you can play them comfortably and relaxed.

Two Beat Bass

Medium

Tommy Flint

* Move the third finger to the fourth string for this one note.

ST. JOSEPH ISLAND BLUES

In this arrangement the thumb plays a two beat bass.

Again the index and middle fingers are used on the melody line.

Be sure to hold the chords.

Tommy Flint

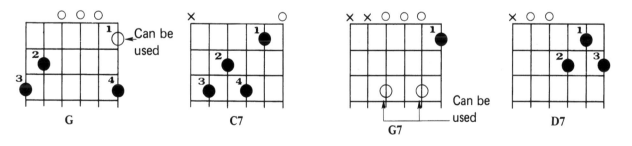

STEADY BASS RHYTHM

This is the foundation of the authentic country finger style blues.
This style should be practiced until it is completely absorbed and the thumb rhythm becomes automatic as a reflex.

Also at this point the basics of the thumb pickin such as muffled bass rhythm, alternate basses, syncopation etc. should be thoroughly reviewed. See page 69.

STEADY THUMPING BLUES
Muffled Basses

Tommy Flint

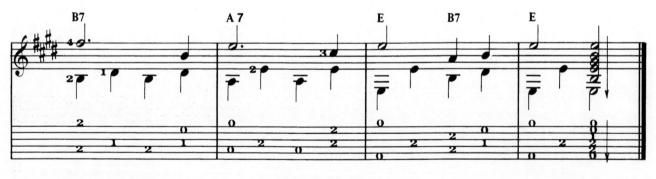

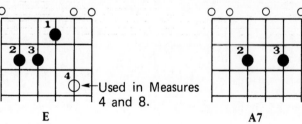

E   A7   B7

At this time it would be wise to review the section on "Syncopation" on page 77 in the Thumb pickin' chapter.

In the following solo the melody notes are played on the count of two and the "and" half way between the counts of three and four.

The index finger can be used to play all of the melody notes. The thumb plays alternate basses.

THE HALF WAY BLUES

Moderately slow

Tommy Flint

111

THE WEST BAY PINES

The melody line is slightly more complex on this page. However the index finger can be used to play all of the melody notes if you wish to do so.

Moderately slow

Tommy Flint

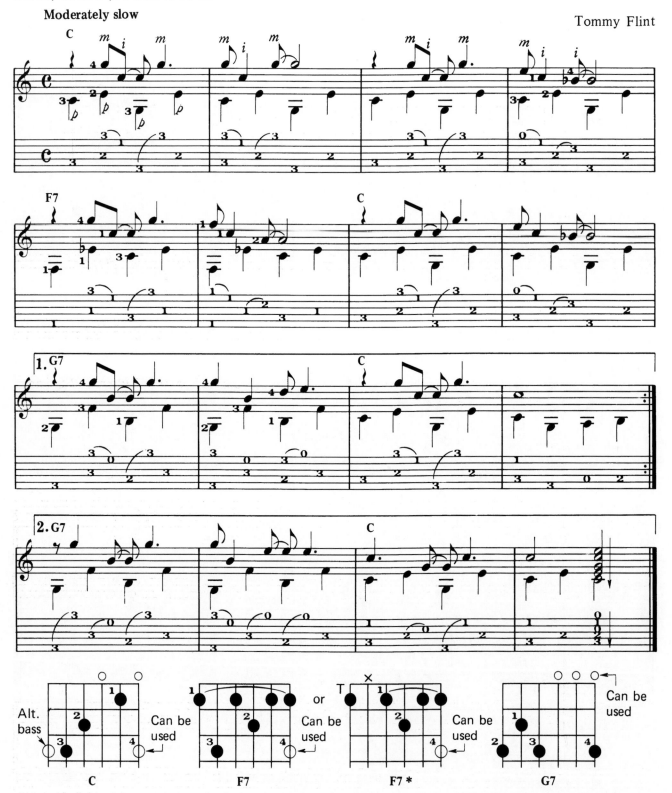

* If you use the thumb to play F7 play the F bass note (1st fret   6 string) on both the first and third beats.

A BLUES RUN

This run can be used as an ending <u>or</u> an intro. When used as an ending to a twelve measure blues, it will begin on the second beat of the eleventh measure and end on the I (tonic) chord in the twelfth measure.

Example

Ending

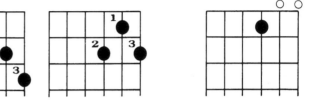

When used as a two measure intro, it will usually begin on the first beat and end on the V7 (dom.7) chord on the third beat of the following measure.

Example

Sometimes pick up notes are used to lead into the intro.

SOME VARIATIONS ON THE RUN

In the following example the third finger is raised to play the first string open.

114

THIS BASIC RUN CAN BE PLAYED IN ANY KEY

Shown below are some examples in the keys of G and A.

The Key of A Run

The following run is in slow triplet rhythm. The thumb plays the chord with a down stroke and the index finger plays the open first string.

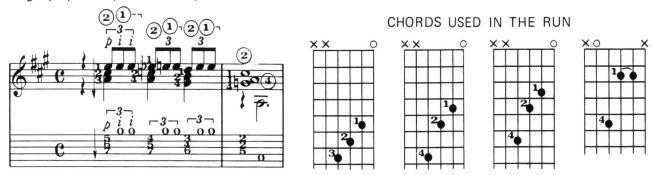

CHORDS USED IN THE RUN

Key of A

In this run the thumb, index and middle fingers are used to play the chord. The thumb plays the open fifth string.

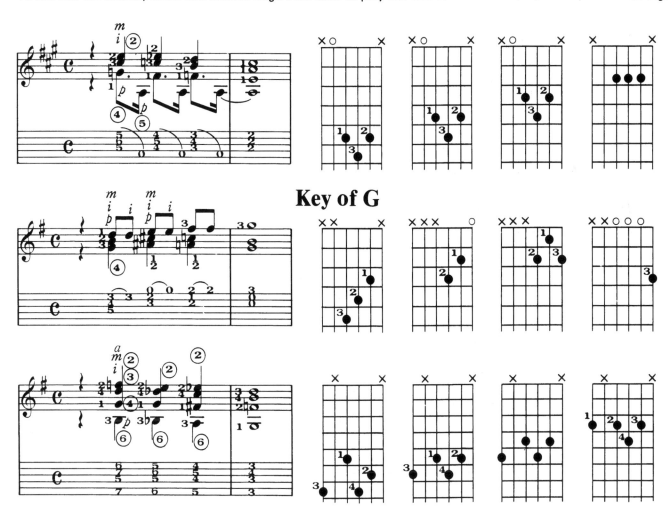

Key of G

THE "HOOK" LICK

This is actually a form of alternate picking. The thumb plays on the beat and the index finger "hooks" or picks the first string between the beats. The strokes are wide apart with a very relaxed feel.

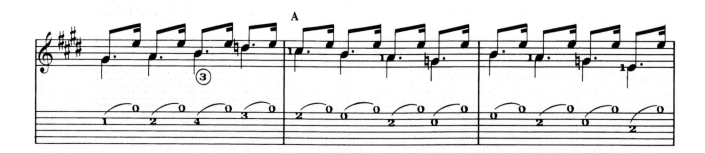

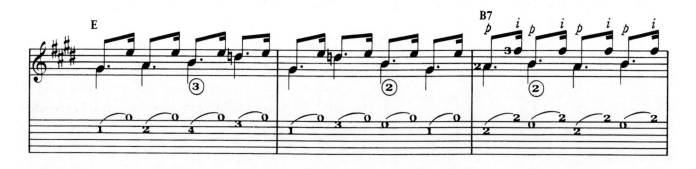

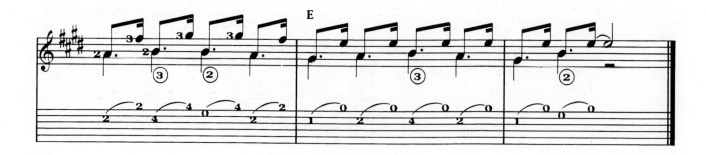

THE "HOOK" LICK WITH A STEADY BASS

In this style the thumb plays a steady muffled bass rhythm as in the previous chapter. The finger "hooks" a note after each beat with the thumb. Use the index finger only. This is very simply alternate picking — thumb-finger-thumb-finger, etc. The strokes are wide apart with a relaxed feel.

Remember   Mel - o - dy   mel - o - dy   mel - o - dy   mel - o - dy

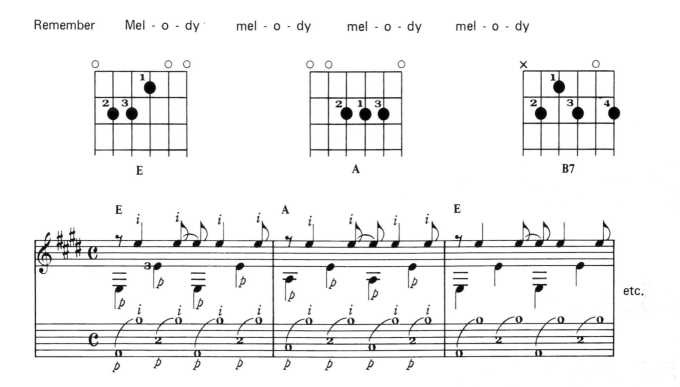

etc.

"Hooking" The Chord

Occasionally the finger may "Hook" more than one string. In the following example the index finger will glide or brush over two or three strings in an upward stroke. The thumb plays a steady muffled bass rhythm.

ect.

117

STEADY HOOKIN' BLUES

This is the same style as described on the previous page with the exception that the index finger may pick either the first <u>or</u> second string.

Tommy Flint

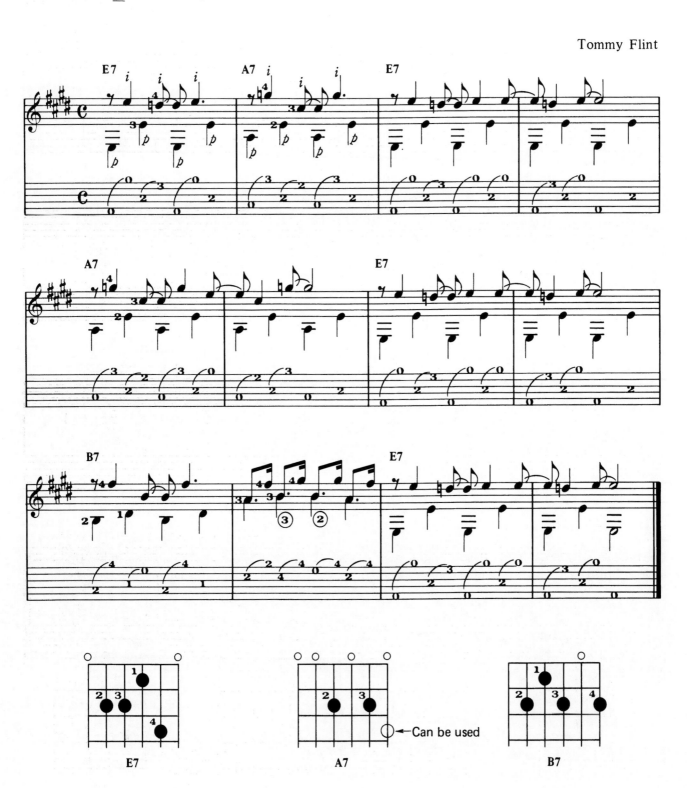

DOWN AND OUT BLUES

In the first three measures raise the first finger and hammer on the third string first fret. (G♯)

Tommy Flint

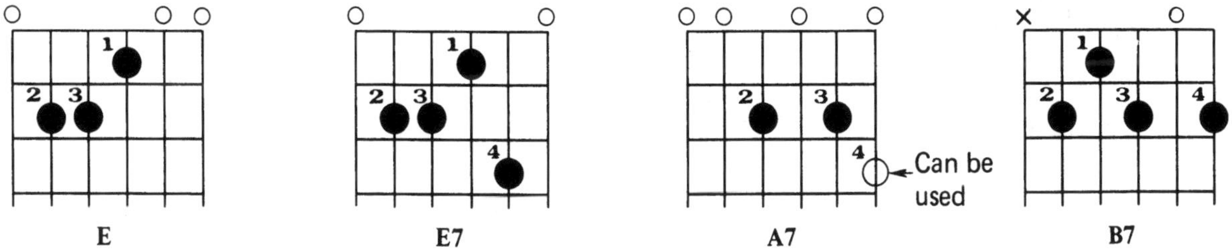

E E7 A7 B7

LONG A BLUES

Some blues guitarist use alternate bass notes. (See page 71 in thumb pickin' chapter.) This is still the muffled bass rhythm. The difference is that the thumb alternates between the fifth and sixth strings.

Tommy Flint

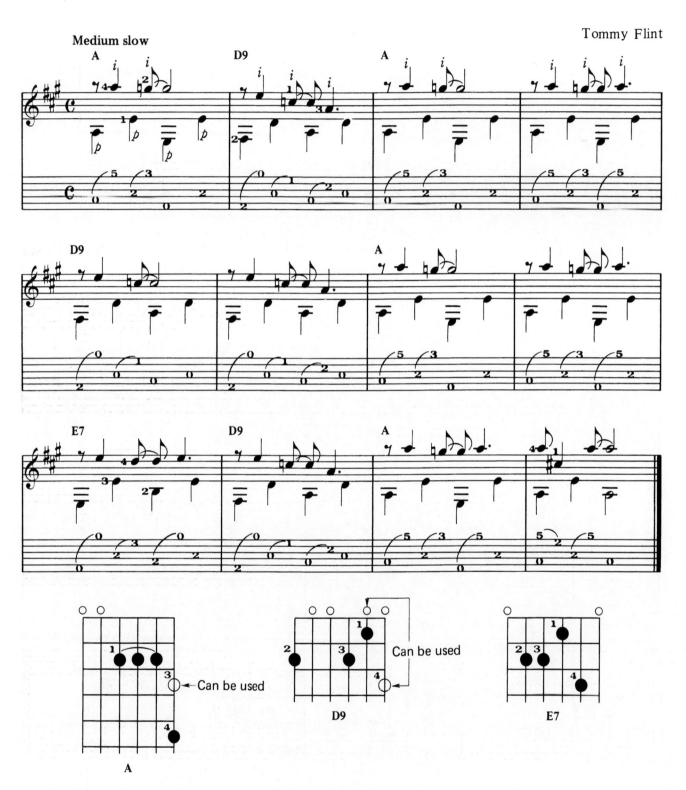

TWO FINGER PICKING WITH A STEADY BASS

When three or more eighth notes are played consecutively on the melody line, alternate picking should be used. When the thumb is playing a steady bass, the index and middle fingers should be used for the alternate picking. Alternate bass rhythm is also used on this page.

The chords are the same as the previous page.

BLUES FOR MOSE

Tommy Flint

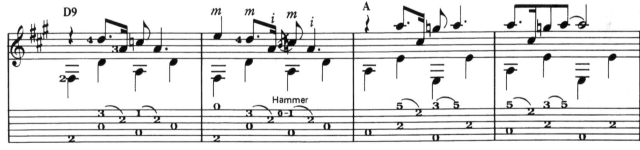

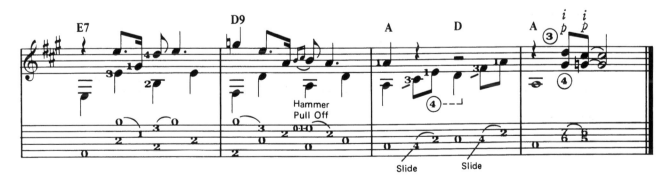

MUHLENBERG COUNTY BLUES

Two finger picking with alternate bass notes.

The Chords Used On This Page

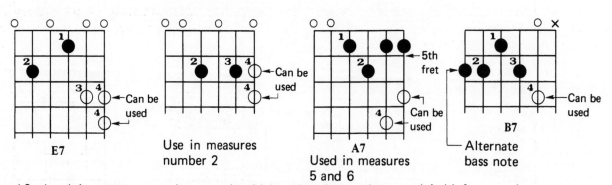

E7

Use in measures number 2

A7
Used in measures 5 and 6

B7

Alternate bass note

The A9 chord in measure number ten should be played as written and held for two beats.

NEW BOX PICKERS BLUES

Tommy Flint

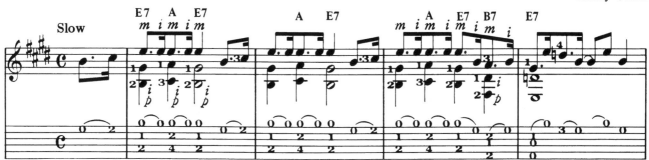

Instructions

In measures number 1,2,3,4,7,8,10,11 and 12 the index and middle fingers alternate on the melody line. The index finger and thumb are used on the two lower notes. Don't muffle the basses. Measures number 5, 6 and 9 are two finger picking with muffled bass.

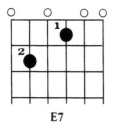

E7

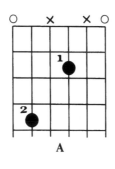

A

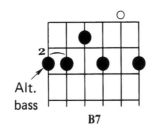

Alt. bass

B7

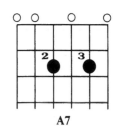

A7

SIXTH INTERVALS

Sixth interval harmony is very effective in playing the blues if used in good taste.

When playing sixth intervals it is necessary to skip a string. For example if the melody is on the first string the harmony will be on the third string, or if the melody is on the second string the harmony will be on the fourth etc. There are two sets of fingerings which are shown below.

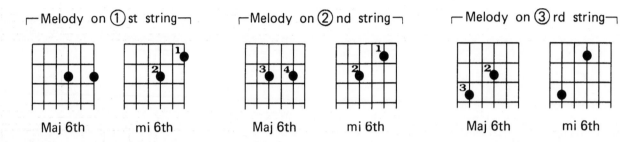

Shown below are some of the most commonly used scales in sixth intervals.

KEY OF C

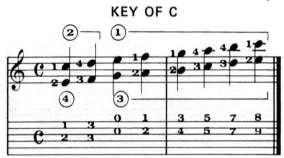

KEY OF D

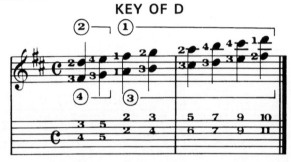

KEY OF E

An E run with some blues intervals.

DUSTY ROAD BLUES
Sixth Interval Harmony

Tommy Flint

On the following page the pick up notes can be played as single notes as shown below.

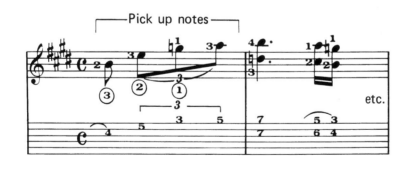

Location of pick up notes.

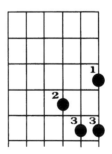

* Fill in: this is not part of the melody but a "Lick" to fill in the long open space.

MEAN AND LOW-DOWN BLUES

Although the rhythm (counting) is more complex than the previous solo, this is still basically sixth interval harmony with blues runs and interspersed with chords.

Tommy Flint

MIDNIGHT RAIN

In the following solo the open string bass notes are sustained below the melody throughout the entire piece. The thumb is used to play the bass notes. The index and middle fingers are used to play the melody and sixth interval harmony.

Tommy Flint

THE SIXTEEN MEASURE BLUES

Up to this point, all the solos have been the standard twelve measure blues. Another standard but less common blues form is the sixteen measure pattern. Shown below are three of the most common sixteen measure blues progressions.

Progression Number 1

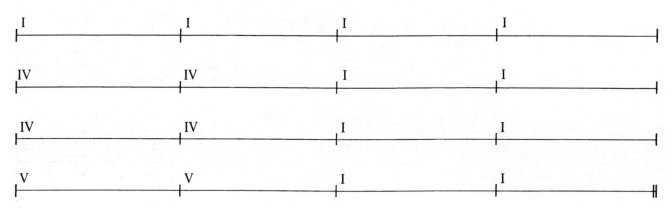

Progression Number 2

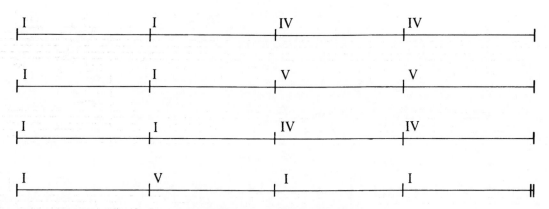

Progression Number 3

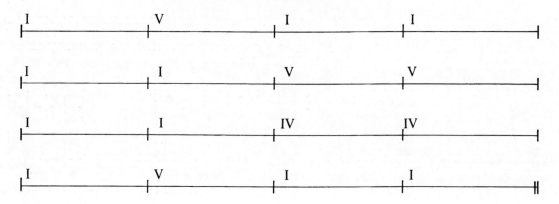

SIXTEEN MILES
A Sixteen Measure Blues

The index finger can be used to play all of the melody note if you prefer this.

Tommy Flint

* If you use the thumb to play F9 play the F bass (1st fret 6 string) on both the first and third beats.

SWAMP WATER BLUES
Sixteen Measure Blues

Tommy Flint

CARELESS LOVE
Sixteen Measure Blues

⑥ string D
⑤ string G

Open string tunings can be very useful in playing the blues. Open string tunings will be explored further in a later chapter.

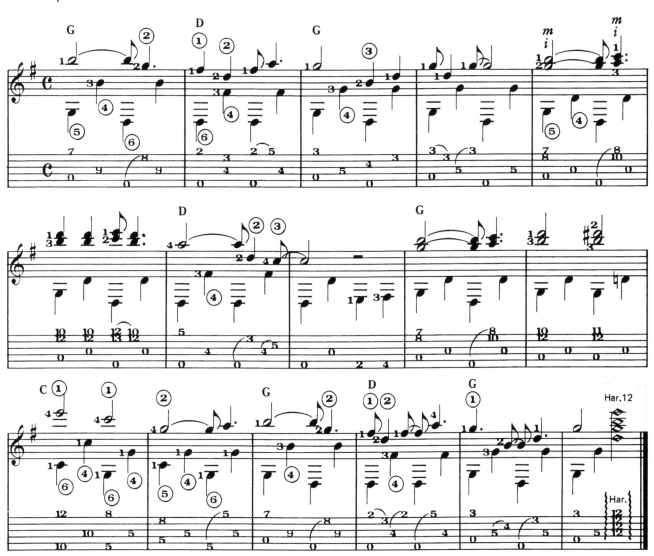

In measures number 5, 6, 9, and 10 no chords are used. The melody and harmony are played in third intervals and the bass strings are played open.

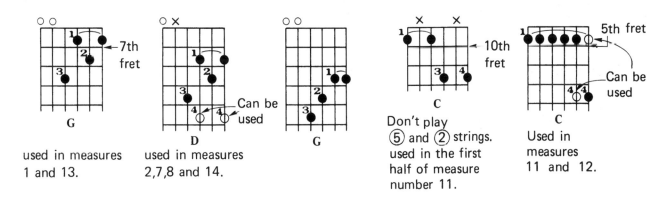

G
used in measures 1 and 13.

D
used in measures 2,7,8 and 14.

G

C
Don't play ⑤ and ② strings. used in the first half of measure number 11.

C
Used in measures 11 and 12.

SINGLE STRING BLUES

It would be a good idea to review the "Blues Scale" on page 106 before playing this solo. All notes can be plucked with the thumb.

STRING ALONG BLUES

Medium

Tommy Flint

Can be played this way

Again this solo is based on the "Blues Scale". In measures number two, five and six the strings should be barred at the third fret and all notes are played legato. Pay close attention to the slides and slurs and try to play with expression.

SOUTH SIDE BLUES

Tommy Flint

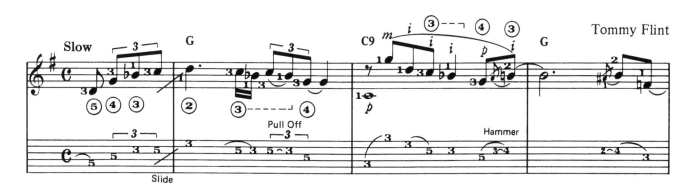

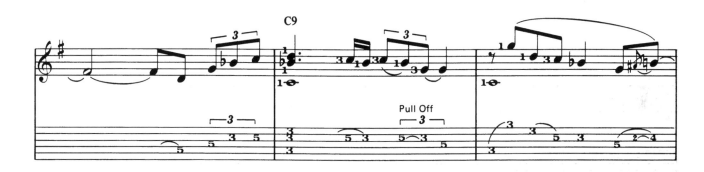

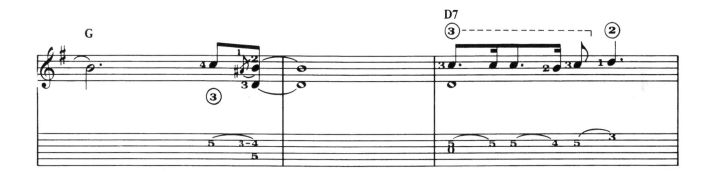

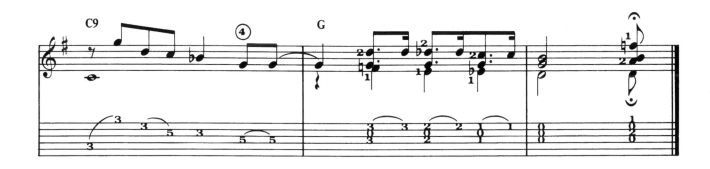

THE BEND

The **Bend** was explained earlier in the "Thumb Pickin" chapter. When the thumb is playing rhythm on the bass strings, the bend is played on the treble strings, usually with the fourth finger and in most cases is no more than a quarter tone. (½ way between frets.)

However the **Bend** described in this chapter is the single string bend and is usually one half to one whole tone (one fret or two frets). For example, to execute the whole tone bend, play G note on the first string (3rd fret) and bend the string until it sounds the same as A on the same string (5th fret.)

The upward bend will be indicated by a curved line above the note. The numeral or fraction above the line indicates how far the string is bent. ½ bend ½ tone (1 fret) 1 bend 1 whole tone (2 frets). Light gauge strings are much easier to bend than regular.

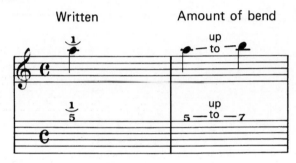

The **downward bend** will be indicated by the downward curved line ⌢ . The string is bent to the desired pitch (½ or 1 tone) before it is plucked. As soon as the string is plucked the pressure of the left hand is released until the string returns to its normal pitch. Again, the number above the curved line indicates the length of the bend.

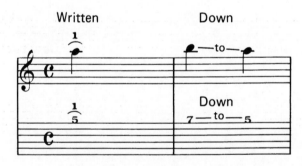

The slow bend will be indicated by a curved line between the notes (or between the numbers in tablature) and the word "Bend" written above. The slow bend may be either up or down.

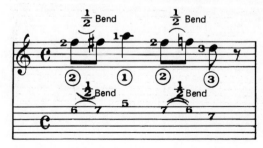

In authentic finger style blues the ½ tone and 1 tone bends are used rather infrequently. The quarter tone bend as described in the "Thumb Pickin" section is much more common.

134

RIGHT AROUND THE BEND

Tommy Flint

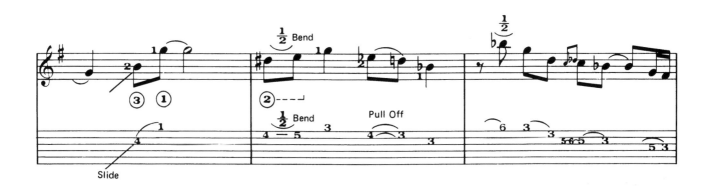

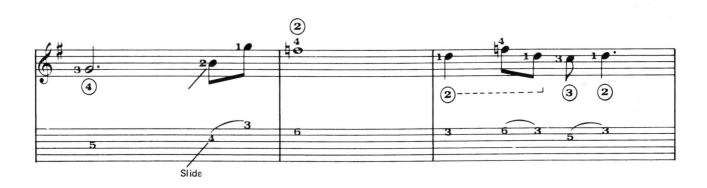

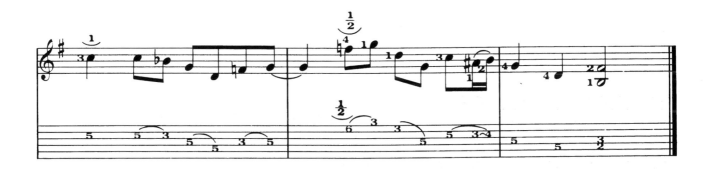

RAGTIME GUITAR

Again, this is not meant to be a history of ragtime guitar. Just as the word "Blues" has been defined in various ways by different people, the term "Ragtime" has various meanings or connotations for different people. (Especially "Ragtime Guitar.") To some it means a form of the Travis Style, or finger style blues. To others it means the music of the twenties, (the tenor banjo.) To still others it recalls the ricky ticky bar room or barrell house piano style, and finally, to some it means the classic form of the Scott Joplin Rags.

This chapter will deal mainly with the classic ragtime. This is usually written A-B-A-C-D with each section repeated. (A:‖B:‖A:‖C:‖D:‖) form. The rhythm is a steady $\frac{2}{4}$ or ¢ with muffled basses, sometimes using alternate bass notes. This is basically the same as Travis style. However the melody line is different. Instead of the widely spaced eighth note swing of the blues, the eighth notes are spaced evenly, exactly the same, distance apart. This creates a piano feel or mood. The melody is also richly syncopated. So, we can now say that ragtime guitar is a syncopated melody played over a stedy "oom pah" rhythm with a piano feel.

A RAGTIME EXERCISE

This is very similar to the steady bass style in the previous chapter. The thumb should play a steady muffled bass rhythm. However, the eighth notes in the melody line should be spaced evenly instead of the wide apart swing feel used in the blues.

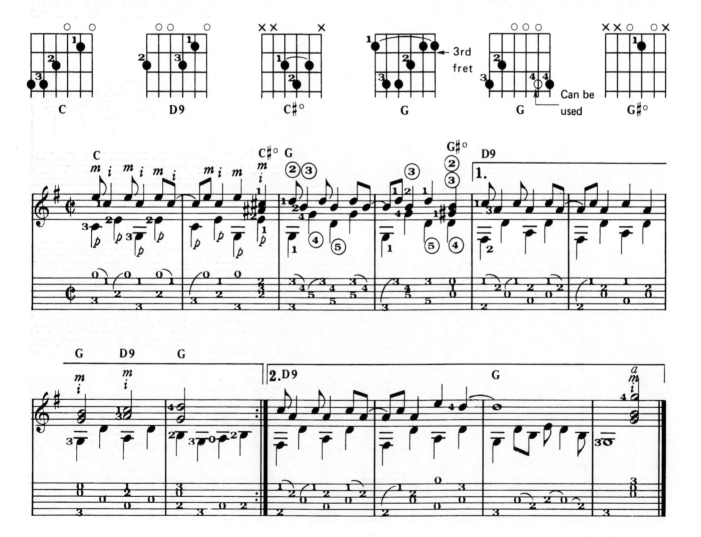

136

The next four solos can be combined and played consecutively as one solo. They should then be played in this order. A:‖ B:‖ A:‖ C:‖ D:‖. The title is "The Classic Rag".

RAINBOW RAG

Tommy Flint

The chords used in this solo are shown on the following page.

TRILLIUM RAG

Tommy Flint

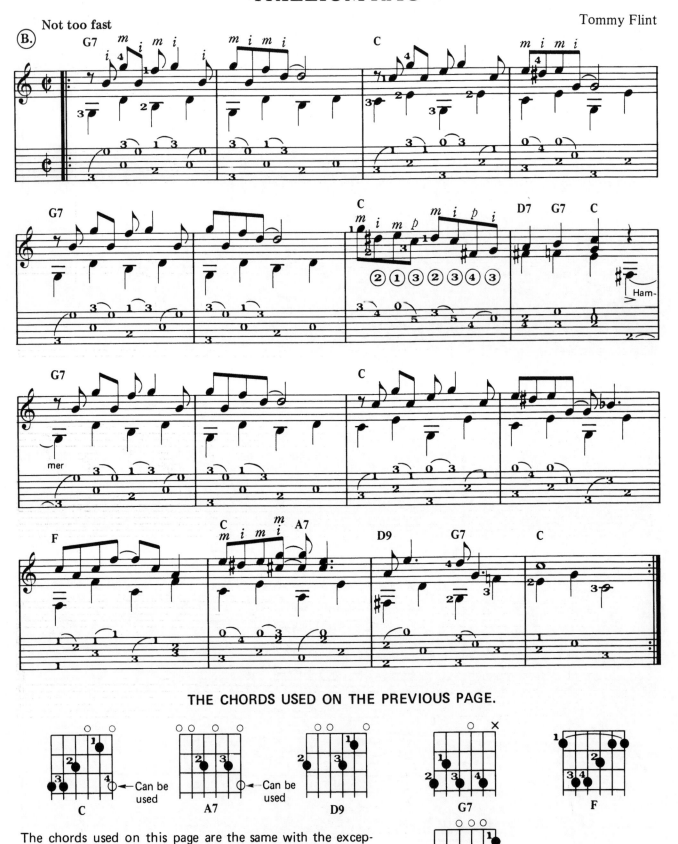

THE CHORDS USED ON THE PREVIOUS PAGE.

The chords used on this page are the same with the exception of the G7 used in measures 1,2,5,6,9 and 10.

QUEEN ANNE'S LACE

Tommy Flint

The only new chord on this page is   Bb

139

PIPSISSEWA

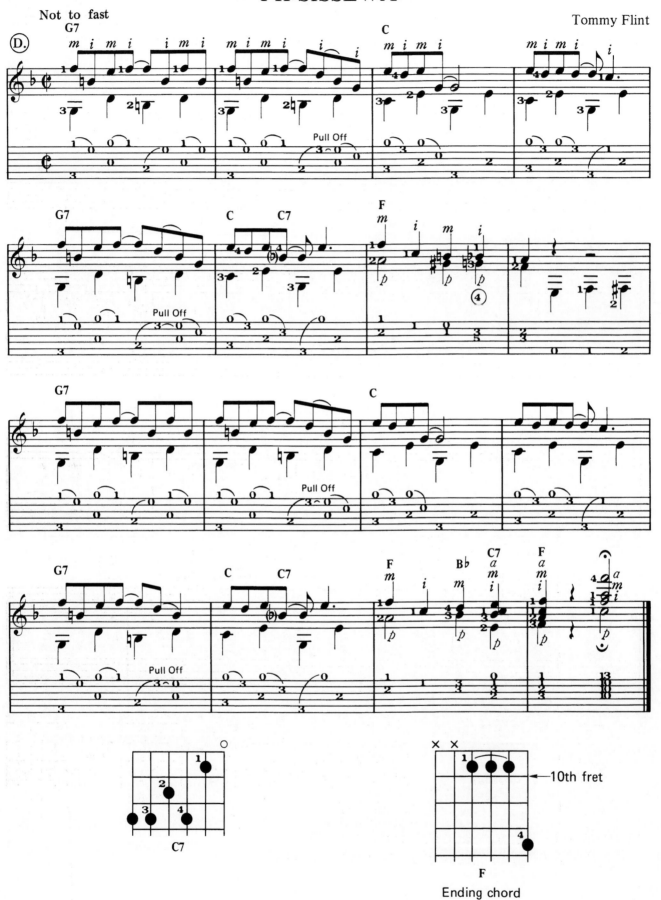

THE ENTERTAINER

Scott Joplin
Arr. by Tommy Flint

This solo shows how it is possible to achieve the steady rhythm feel without the constant thumb strokes.

Am-5

D9

C7
Used in measure
number.13.

Fmaj7   3rd fret   Can be used

Fm6   3rd fret

G7

The C, C7 and F chords are standard fingering

See Mel Bay's COUNTRY RAGTIME GUITAR by Tommy Flint

"HOE DOWN" PICKING

This style is used to play tunes that are usually associated with the flat pick such as fast fiddle tunes, Hoe downs, Jazz lines etc. If you are interested in this type of music, it is important that you become reasonably proficient in single string picking. With practice and persistance it is possible to obtain speed comparable to the fastest flat picking guitarist.

The following symbols will be used for this style.

⊓ = Down stroke. Use the thumb.

V = Up stroke. Use the index finger.

You should strive to obtain the same quality (or timbre) of tone on both down and up stroke. At first it will be difficult to produce a good "big" tone with the finger, but with practice this can be achieved.

The following example, which is the C major scale, should be practiced slowly at first, making certain that all of the notes are spaced evenly. Tap your foot on every count. The thumb should play on the tap when the foot is down. When the foot is raised, the the index finger should play the up stroke.

Example

Stroke	⊓ V ⊓ V ⊓ V ⊓ V
Foot	Tap-up-Tap-up-Tap-up-Tap-up
Count	1 & 2 & 3 & 4 &

Eighth Notes

Count 1 & 2 & 3 & 4 &
Foot   tap up tap up tap up tap up

Eighth Notes

Count 1 & 2 & 3 & 4 &
Foot   tap up tap up tap up tap up

142

SINGLE STRING PICKING EXERCISES
Sixteenth Notes

There are four notes on each beat or each tap of the foot. Technically sixteenth notes are twice as fast as eighth notes so consequently, the picking will be doubled. Instead of counting One-and-Two-and say Cat-er-pill-er—Cat-er-pill-er. This sounds strange but is a very effective method of keeping time.

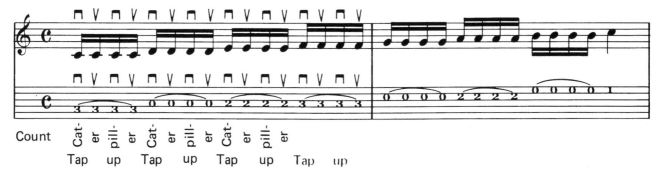

Eight And Sixteenths

These are played the same as sixteenth notes with the second note omitted from each group.

Count Cat-pill-er or One-and-a

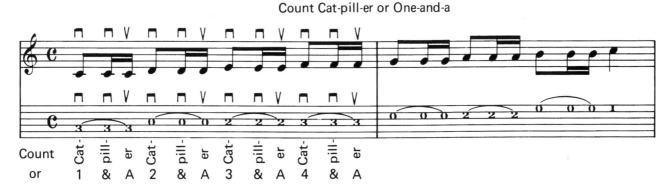

Sixteenth And Eighth

These are played the same as sixteenth notes with the fourth note omitted from each group. Count Cat-a-pill-Cat-a-pill-or One-a-and-Two-a-and etc.

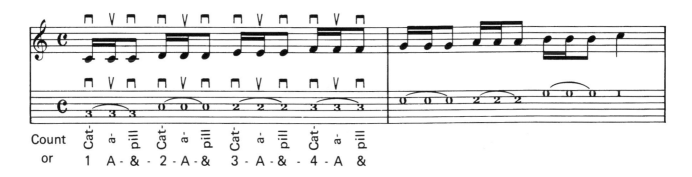

143

THE EIGHTH OF JANUARY

BUFFALO GALS

Moderately bright

145

MOVABLE SCALES

By using scales with no open strings it is possible to play in any key by moving to a higher or lower position on the fingerboard. Also, playing the scales in various rhythms or picking patterns is an excellent method of developing speed and control in single string picking. Shown below are two of the most commonly used scales. All scales should be memorized and played until thoroughly mastered.

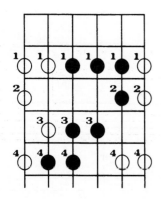

SCALE NO. 1

Showing five notes of the lower register and four notes of the higher register. (white circles.) The black circles show one one octave.

Learn the scale in all keys.

The chart below shows the notes on the fifth and sixth strings to the twelfth fret.

The scale no.2 chart shows the G scale. The first note of the scale is on the third fret sixth string. To play the A scale simply start on the fifth fret sixth string and use the same fingering.

SCALE NO. 1

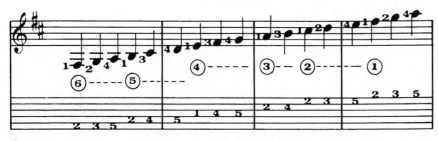

SCALE NO. 2

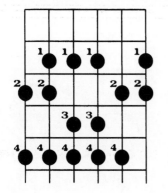

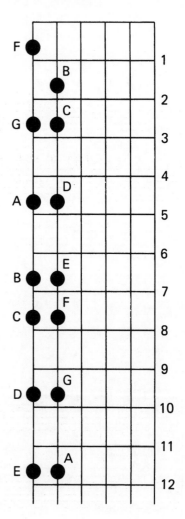

SINGLE STRING SPEED BUILDER

The following exercises can be practiced to develop coordination and control and to build speed.

Scales number one and two should be played in all keys using the following rhythms.

Eighth Notes

Count   1 & 2 & 3 & 4 &
Foot   Tap Tap Tap Tap

Sixteenth Notes

The sixteenth notes should be practiced to obtain the true Hoe-Down or fiddle tune feel.

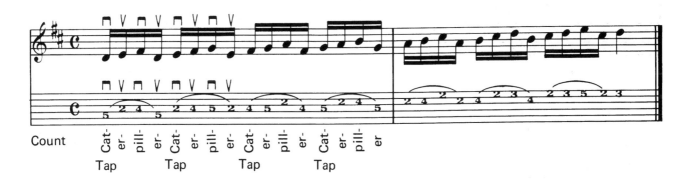

Count   Cat- er- pill- er- Cat- er- pill- er- Cat- er- pill- er- Cat- er- pill- er
       Tap   Tap   Tap   Tap

Triplets

This is still alternate picking. However, because there are three notes in each group the picking is reversed on each group.

147

$\frac{6}{8}$ PICKING

The following solo should be memorized and then played in various keys using scale no 1.

$\frac{6}{8}$ Picking : The method of picking is very similar to playing triplets in $\frac{4}{4}$ time. The picking is reversed on each group. However the picking is still alternate because there are three notes in each group.

PADDY WHACK

IMPRESSION OF RAPID PICKING

The following scales can be used to create the illusion of VERY VERY RAPID PICKING. Only the first note on each string is picked. The other two notes are slurred or hammered. These scales should be practiced in all keys in triplets and eighth notes. They can also be used as connecting scales when changing from a low to to a high position on the fingerboard.

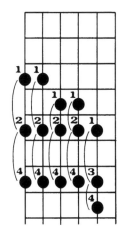

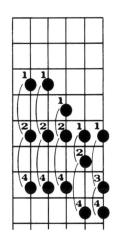

Practice   both scales in thirds in all keys.

Pick the first note in each group. slur the other two.

TRIPLETS

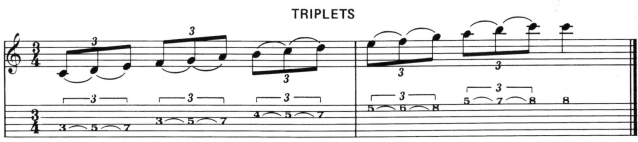

EIGHTH NOTES

DOUBLE STOPS

This is actually harmony in thirds. However, when playing eighth notes, alternate picking should be used. The index and middle fingers will alternate on the higher notes and the thumb will be used on the lower note.

Practice the following scales for speed and accuracy.

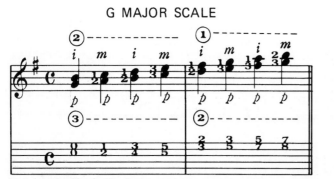

G MAJOR SCALE

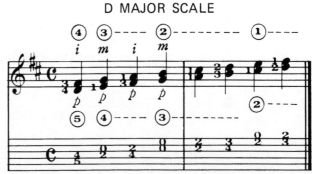

D MAJOR SCALE

AN ENDING

Moderately bright

The following example shows how double string picking can be used to lead into phrases or as fill ins. It is also a very good style to use for hoe-downs but rather difficult.

Brightly

etc.

CHROMATIC PICKING

This style is basically the same as the "Chromatic Banjo" style. The theory is to play as many open strings as possible while fingering the other strings high on the fingerboard. For instance, the third string may sound higher than the open first. Two notes should never be played consecutively on the same string if this can be avoided. If it cannot be avoided, the notes should be slurred. This is a very difficult style for most people and should be practiced slowly at first.

Please observe the fingering, strings and picking very closely.

THE GALWAY PIPER
(The Rakes Of Mallow)

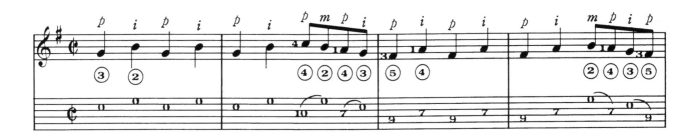

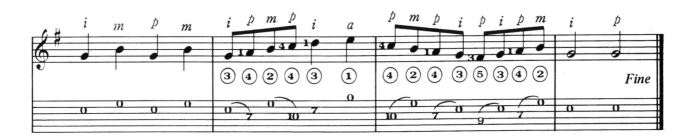

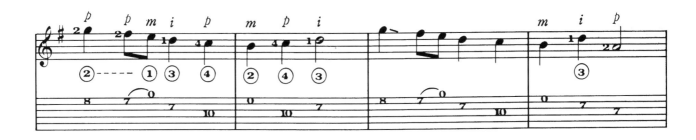

THE PEDAL STEEL GUITAR STYLE

The pedal steel sound can be simulated by changing

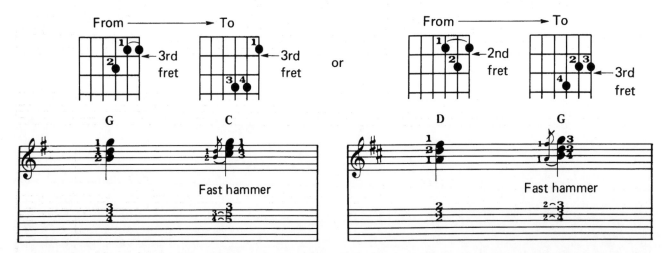

Very Legato. The fingers should remain on G chord after you have changed to C or on D after you have changed to G. The electric guitar is best suited for this style and a volume foot pedal is very helpful.

A Pedal Steel Intro

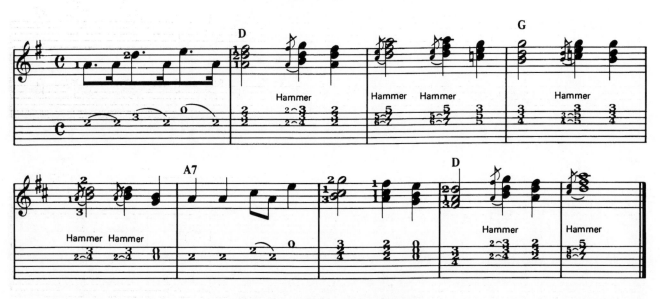

A Pedal Steel Ending

MIDNIGHT IN NASHVILLE
Pedal Steel Guitar Style

Tommy Flint

CHICKEN PICKING

Use light strings to get a "Flappy" sound when the strings come in contact with the finger board.

X = Deaden the string by releasing the pressure of the left hand.

FINGER LICKING GOOD

Tommy Flint

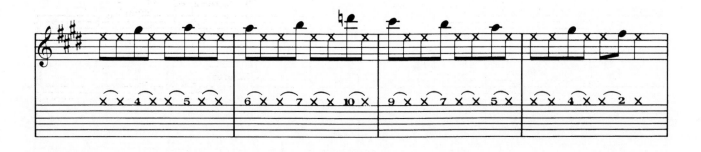

HOW TO PLAY BLUEGRASS BANJO STYLE
ON THE GUITAR

Here is the guitar chord comparable to the 5 string banjo G tuning.

The 5 string banjo is a drone instrument so consequently the G note can be sounded in any of the three principal chords. (G-C-D7) It may be played on the open third string or the first string third fret.

The 2nd and 4th frets on the ③ and ④ strings can be used

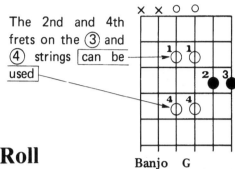

Banjo   G

A Banjo Roll

This Roll Can Be Used As An Ending

Another Roll

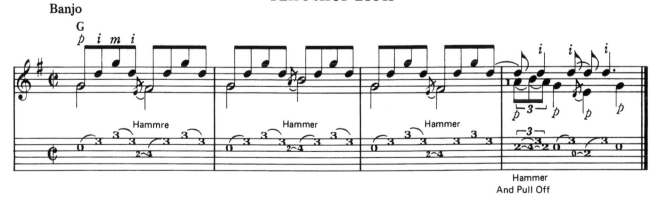

ROUGH RIVER HOE-DOWN
Bluegrass Banjo Style

Tommy Flint

ALTERNATE TUNINGS

Alternate tunings are indispensable tools for many finger style guitarists. They are very practical because the bass strings can be played open and most of the chords are straight barres. Also, because the basses are open, the melody can be played single note or in thirds or sixths. Another good reason for tunings is because some melodies are very difficult to play in the standard tuning and sound much better in one of the alternates. This section will demonstrate some of the most common tunings. Also some unusual ones.

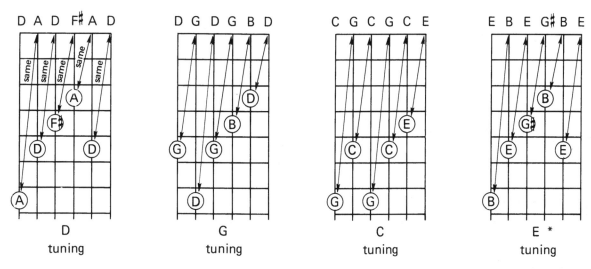

In the following tunings only the bass strings are changed from the standard tuning. The standard chord forms can be used on the first four strings.

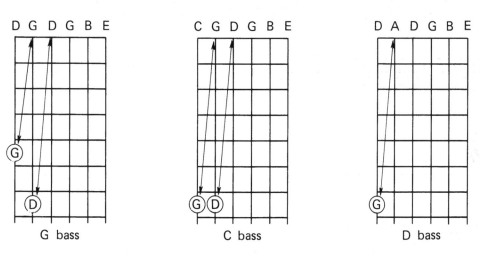

Some Additional Tunings

G minor	D minor	G modal	D modal
6 5 4 3 2 1	6 5 4 3 2 1	6 5 4 3 2 1	6 5 4 3 2 1
D G D G B♭ D	D A D F A D	D G D G C D	D A D G A D
A	A minor	E minor	Lowered 1st
6 5 4 3 2 1	6 5 4 3 2 1	6 5 4 3 2 1	6 5 4 3 2 1
E A E A C♯ E	E A E A C E	E B E G B E	E A D G B D

* When strings are raised lighter gauge strings should be used.

157

HURON COVE
D Tuning

Tommy Flint

THE STRAITS OF MACKINAC
C Tuning

Tommy Flint

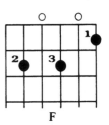

F

Used in measures
4, and 8.

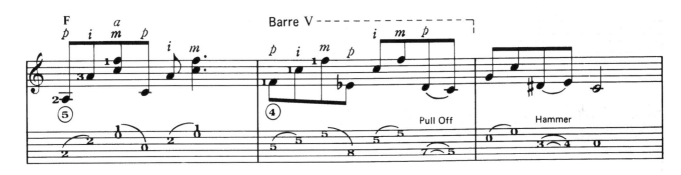

WHIP-POOR-WILL TIME
G Tuning

Tommy Flint

All of the strings in the G chord are open except the first string which is used for most of the melody notes.

To play the A chord in measures 3, 4, 11 and 12 bar all six strings at the second fret. Use the third and fourth fingers to play additional melody notes.

The D chord in measures 5, 6, 13 and 14 is a straight bar chord at the seventh fret. Use the second, third and fourth fingers to add the melody notes.

The C chord in measure 15 is a straight barre at the fifth fret.

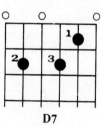

D7

Used in
measure 8

Printed in Great Britain
by Amazon.co.uk, Ltd.,
Marston Gate.